# A POPULAR DICTIONARY OF HINDUISM

*By the same author*

YOGA AND INDIAN PHILOSOPHY

THE HERITAGE OF THE VEDES

YOGA, ITS BEGINNINGS AND DEVELOPMENT

THE YOGI AND THE MYSTIC

STUDIES IN INDIAN AND COMPARATIVE MYSTICISM (ED.)

SYMBOLS IN ART AND RELIGION: THE INDIAN AND THE COMPARATIVE PERSPECTIVES (ED.)

DHAMMAPADAM: THE WAY TO TRUTH (IN CZECH)

LOVE DIVINE: STUDIES IN BHAKTI AND DEVOTIONAL MYSTICISM (ED.)

# A Popular Dictionary of Hinduism

Karel Werner

CURZON PRESS

First published in 1994 in the United Kingdom by
Curzon Press Ltd., Church Road, Richmond, Surrey TW9 2QA

ISBN 0 7007 0279 2



**British Library Cataloguing in Publication Data**
A Catalogue record for this book is available from the British Library



Printed by Redwood Books., Wiltshire

# ABBREVIATIONS

| | |
|---|---|
| adj. | adjective |
| AU | Aitareya Upaniṣad |
| Av. | Avesta, Avestan |
| AV | Atharva Veda |
| BhG | Bhagavad Gītā |
| BP | Bhāgavata Purāṇa |
| BS | Brahma Sūtras of Bādarāyaṇa |
| BU | Bṛhadāraṇyaka Upaniṣad |
| cf. | compare |
| CU | Chāndogya Upaniṣad |
| f. | feminine |
| fr. | from |
| Germ. | Germanic |
| Gr. | Greek |
| IE | Indo-European |
| Lat. | Latin |
| lit. | literally |
| Lith. | Lithuanian |
| m. | masculine |
| Mhb | Mahābhārata |
| n. | neuter |
| Pkt. | Prakrit |
| Pl. | Pāli |
| pl. | plural |
| RV | Ṛg Veda |
| SB | Śatapatha Brāhmaṇa |
| sg. | singular |
| Skt. | Sanskrit |
| Slav. | Slavonic |
| SV | Sāma Veda |
| TS | Taittirīya Saṁhitā |
| vern. | vernacular |
| VS | Vājasaneyi Saṁhitā |
| YV | Yajur Veda |

# PREFACE

The initial words of most entries in this dictionary are in Sanskrit or a vernacular or derived from one or the other. Some entries start with proper names and a relatively small number of entries begins with an English word which expresses a concept relevant to Hinduism. The following rules have been applied:

(1) English words at the beginning of entries are written with an initial capital letter, and so are all proper names.

(2) Sanskrit and vernacular words are written in *italics* throughout, and with a small initial letter as is customary in dictionaries. (This corresponds to the usage in Sanskrit texts, since the *devanāgarī* alphabet does not have capital letters.)

(3) Sanskrit proper names are written with initial capitals to comply with rule (1), and they are not italicized, e.g. 'Caitanya'. That includes the names of schools of philosophy and of sectarian movements, e.g. 'Advaita Vedānta' or 'Brāhmo Samāj', some titles, e.g. Svāmi, and the titles of Sanskrit works which are a part of the Hindu scriptures or traditional literature, e.g. 'Chāndogya Upaniṣad'. Only titles of works of individual authors have been italicized, e.g. Madhva's *Sarvadarśaṇasaṅgraha*.

(4) Diacritical marks have been applied to all Sanskrit and vernacular words throughout in keeping with the generally accepted method of transliterating the *devanāgarī* alphabet. This includes names of gods, e.g. Kṛṣṇa, but excludes Indian personal names and some other types of proper name where English spelling has become customary, e.g. Ramakrishna, Bombay etc.

(5) Entries are in alphabetical order according to the English alphabet but it should be noted that the Sanskrit alphabet has two extra sibilants, 'ś' and 'ṣ', and Sanskrit words starting with these letters are placed in this dictionary *after*

entries starting with 's'. When correctly pronounced, 'ś' and 'ṣ' differ from each other, but the difference can be disregarded for the purposes of this dictionary, as indicated in the note on pronunciation. (The reader is reminded that some authors writing on Indian subjects in English use inconsistent simplified forms of transliteration of Sanskrit words and often fail to discriminate between the two extra sibilants, transliterating both of them as 'sh'. This may confuse the meaning in some cases and it has the additional disadvantage in dictionaries in that it leads to altered sequence of entries, especially among those starting with the letter 's'.)

ACKNOWLEDGEMENT

In compiling this dictionary I was greatly helped by my wife Marian who patiently read through its draft several times, corrected spelling and typing mistakes and made valuable suggestions with respect to the wording, style and even the contents of many entries.

# A NOTE ON THE PRONUNCIATION OF THE SANSKRIT ALPHABET

The Sanskrit alphabet is phonetical: all vowels and consonants are pronounced clearly and always in the same way.

**Vowels**:

| | |
|---|---|
| a | short like 'u' in 'luck' |
| ā | long like 'a' in 'grass' |
| i | short like 'i' in 'sit' |
| ī | long like 'ee' in 'sweet' |
| u | short like 'u' in 'bull' |
| ū | long like 'oo' in 'food' |
| ṛ | as a hard rolling syllable-producing vowel 'rr' (perhaps the only living IE language which has preserved this vowel is Czech, e.g. in 'brk'; the new Indian pronunciation is 'ri' as in 'river' and this has also been adopted in English pronunciation and spelling of some words, e.g. 'Sanskrit') |
| e | long like 'ai' in 'fair' |
| o | long like 'au' in 'cause' |
| ai | like 'i' in 'mine', i.e. as a diphthong |
| au | like 'ou' in 'house', i.e. as a diphthong |

**Consonants**:

| | |
|---|---|
| k | like 'c' in 'comma' |
| kh | like 'k-h' in 'cook-house' |
| g | like 'g' in 'giggle' |
| gh | like 'g-h' in 'log-house' |
| ṅ | like 'ng' in 'thing' |
| c | like 'ch' in 'chalk' |
| ch | like 'ch-h' in 'church-house' |
| j | like 'j' in 'jam' |
| jh | like 'dgeh' in 'Edgehill' |
| ṅ | like 'gn' in Italian 'signor' |

## Note on pronunciation

| | |
|---|---|
| t, ṭ | like 't' in 'tea' |
| th, ṭh | like 't-h' in 'hot-house' |
| d, ḍ | like 'd' in 'day' |
| dh, ḍh | like 'd-h' in 'god-head' |
| n, ṇ | like 'n' in 'now' |
| p | like 'p' in 'pot' |
| ph | like 'p-h' in 'top-heavy' |
| b | like 'b' in 'bow' |
| bh | like 'b-h' in 'sub-heading' |
| m | like 'm' in 'mum' |
| y | like 'y' in 'yard' |
| r | like 'r' in 'red', but rolled (as in Scotland) |
| l | like 'l' in 'law' |
| v | like 'v' in 'valid' |
| ś, ṣ | like 'sh' in 'show' |
| s | like 'ss' in 'assess' |
| h, ḥ | like 'h' in 'house' |
| ṁ | similar to 'ng' in 'thing', but only slightly nasalized |

Strictly speaking, there is a difference between the pronunciation of consonants with and without diacritical marks (e.g. d, ḍ) and those with different diacritical marks (ś, ṣ), but it is rather subtle and can for all practical purposes be disregarded.

# INTRODUCTION

Hinduism is perhaps the most complicated religious phenomenon in the world. Indeed, views have been expressed that it is not one religion, but many, a kind of coalition of religions. On the other hand, there are some features within Hinduism which bind together the apparently bewildering variety of its deities, cults, customs, spiritual practices, beliefs, sectarian teachings and philosophical schools and which have provided a strong sense of religious belonging as well as of social and cultural togetherness for the peoples of India across linguistic and racial barriers throughout their long history, despite many changes in the political scene.

One reason for the complexity of Hinduism is the fact that it has no known starting-point and no single charismatic figure who could be regarded as its originator. It took shape over a period of many hundreds of years and many diverse influences left their mark on its fabric. It is therefore by following, at least in brief outline, the historical sequences and developments in the religious scene which led to the emergence of Hinduism as a religious system that we can hope to start appreciating its many facets and the way they form a multifarious yet coherent whole. There are several clearly recognizable phases in the historical development of Hinduism:

1. **The riddle of Harappan religion**. A great civilization flourished in the Indus valley and adjacent areas in the third millennium B.C. While its writing still awaits decipherment, the archaeological finds testify to a highly developed and stratified religious system. The nature of the burials indicates a belief in the continuation of life. Numerous female figurines, some of them suggesting pregnancy, point to a cult of the Great Goddess, perhaps the Great Mother of the Universe (known as Aditi to the Vedas and under various forms of the Devī in later Hinduism). Depictions of a male

deity as surrounded by animals remind one of the Hindu god Śiva as Paśupati, his meditative position is reminiscent of Śiva's role as the great Yogi (Yogapati) and his three faces might suggest a trinitarian view of the deity akin to the Purāṇic Trimūrti. The ithiphallic feature of this deity and finds of phallic emblems further point to the role of the *liṅga* in Śaivite cults. Other connections could be pointed out as a result of a detailed analysis of Harappan pictures on seals by comparison with Hindu mythology.

2. **The Indo-European prehistory**. The Indo-Āryans reached India in the second millennium B.C. in several waves of immigration over a period of several hundred years, after a long and slow migration from Eastern Europe. There they had for a long time been a part of the great IE family of tribes with whom they shared a common language and culture, as is obvious from similarities which survived both the parting of this family into tribes and their migrations and development into separate nations. The Vedic religion of the Indo-Āryans shows a number of parallels with the Greek, Roman, Celtic, Slavonic, Germanic and other ancient IE religions. Besides the gods, of whom the 'Heavenly Father' (Vedic Dyaus Pitar, Gr. Zeus Pater, and Lat. Jupiter) is the best known, there are concepts such as 'destiny', 'fate', 'retribution', 'necessity' or 'cosmic order', and ideas about the afterlife, including the belief in re-incarnation (metempsychosis) and immortality or the final salvation. A careful comparative investigation of these concepts would show how much of what Hinduism stands for has IE roots.

3. **The Vedic vision of the world**. Once in India, the Indo-Āryans further elaborated and consolidated their religious heritage by codifying it, by 1000 B.C., in the collection of hymns known as the Ṛg Veda. Its authorship is ascribed to generations of inspired seers (*ṛṣis*) – poets, visionaries, mystics and philosophers as well as spiritual leaders and moral guides of their communities. They developed a global picture of the cosmos, its beginnings and its duration as governed by the cosmic law (*ṛta*) on all levels – physical, social, ethical and spiritual. In order to convey

their insights in an effective way to the people, they translated them into regular re-enactments of the drama of creation and of the struggle between the forces of life and stagnation or decay through the use of symbolic rituals, both private and communal, and through religious festivals. In this way the lives of individuals, families and communities were regulated. The interplay of cosmic and social forces and their impact on human life was further reflected in the richness of myths and legends with the gods, divine heroes, demons and other supernatural beings as principal actors who could be propitiated and won over to grant prosperity. For those who thought further ahead there were the means of securing heaven after death in the company of blessed forefathers, and those with higher aspirations could even attempt to tread the path to immortality discovered by the greatest among the ancient *ṛṣis*, thereby becoming exempt from the normal human lot of successive lives. This stage of Indo-Āryan religion is often called Vedism.

4. **The Brahminic universe of ritual action**. As is only natural with human communities, the majority of Vedic people focused their interest on prosperity on earth and at best on securing heavenly rewards in the afterlife without giving much thought to their final destiny. Their expectations were catered for by the successors of the *ṛṣis*, the guardians of the sacred lore codified in the Ṛg Veda, who developed into a hereditary caste of priests (brahmins). They succeeded in gaining a high reputation as indispensable experts in ritual communication with the deities and cosmic forces. They compiled two further Vedic collections, the Sāma Veda and the Yajur Veda, mainly for their liturgical procedures, and elaborated theories about the correspondences between ritual action and cosmic processes which have come down to us in books known as the Brāhmaṇas. Their confidence in their own skill and in the efficacy of rituals, performed at specially erected altars in the open, was such that there was nothing which, in their view, a correctly performed rite could not bring about. This obviously rather externalized form of religion known as Brāhmanism had its heyday at a time (cca

900–600 B.C.) when the Indo-Āryan civilization was expanding and materially prospering.

5. **The Upaniṣadic *gnosis***. The Brahminic ritualism tended to grow out of proportion and was eventually felt by many to be a burden. Thoughtful individuals began to realize that behind its formalism there was not the true spiritual force which once had expressed itself in the inspired hymns that now were endlessly repeated by the brahmins as mere liturgical formulas. A new spiritual search for direct experience of the transcendent divine reality, helped by the existence of hermits and wandering ascetics outside or alongside the Vedic tradition who were given to contemplation rather than to ritual, led to a revival of the mystic vision of the ancient seers. This time its results were expressed not in hymnic poetry, but in the philosophical language of the Upaniṣads. (The earliest of them became the last section of the Vedic scriptures and came to be recognized as revelation or divinely inspired.)

   Besides some spiritually-minded brahmins the bearers of this rediscovered wisdom were members of other classes, among them often aristocratic *kṣatriyas*, including a few kings. The great Upaniṣadic sages found the solution to the riddle of life and its goal in the discovery of the essential identity of one's inner self (*ātman*) with the divine source of the whole universe (*brahman*). The direct knowledge of this identity, best expressed for us by the Greek word *gnosis*, results according to them in liberation from rebirth which amounts to the final salvation. It cannot be secured by purely religious piety and observance, because they lead only to a temporary respite in heavenly abodes followed sooner or later by further births in lower realms of *saṁsāra*.

6. **Movements outside the Vedic tradition**. The goal of final liberation (*mokṣa*) was never entirely lost sight of by some of those who lived outside or dropped out of the established Vedic civilization with its cult-orientated priesthood. Among these outsiders were, in the first place, Vrātyas, a loose oath-bound alliance of Indo-Āryan tribal fraternities who were the earliest invaders of India and moved eastwards to Magadha

when further immigrants arrived in large numbers and settled in Saptasindhu. The Vrātyas possessed a wealth of magic, mystic and speculative lore which only partly overlapped with that of the Vedic *ṛṣis*. It was not compiled into a collection until around 600 B.C. when the Vedic civilization overran also the Vrātya territory and brahmins made selective use of Vrātya materials to create the Atharva Veda. In it some of the Upaniṣadic insights are foreshadowed, while its less elevated magic elements and some of its ritual practices also contributed to the future shape of Hinduism.

Further influences, on a higher level, came from solitary sages and wanderers, some known even from early references in the Ṛg Veda (*munis*, *keśins*), who rejected life in society in their pursuit of liberation. There were among them ascetics (*śramaṇas*); yogis practising a variety of techniques, among them meditational absorption (*dhyāna*); and even speculative philosophers. Some of them acquired a high reputation and circles of disciples gathered around them in their forest schools. Around 500 B.C. there emerged from this background two highly influential movements, namely Jainism and Buddhism. They almost obliterated for several hundred years the Brahminic grip on society, partly also as a result of royal patronage, especially under the Maurya dynasty whose founder, Chandragupta, became a Jain, and its third ruler, Aśoka, an ardent Buddhist. It was Buddhism which then came to dominate many parts of India.

7. **The Brahminic revival and the 'birth' of Hinduism**. All the unorthodox movements catered, in the first place, for those who aspired to personal liberation through the renunciation of worldly involvement and they were based in ascetic communities which in the case of Buddhism gradually developed into monasteries. Therefore there was a considerable gap, both physically and spiritually, between them and their lay followers who were less committed to the immediate effort of reaching the goal of liberation, but found some inspiration in it as a distant prospect, while supporting the monks materially. Brahmins, on the other hand, lived as family men within the community ready to cater for all its religious needs, including those which monks were not

willing to meet, such as officiating at births, marriages and funerals. The previous high authority of the monks in religious matters was, of course, swept aside by the tide of reformist movements and the loss of royal patronage and the confidence of the people, and so the brahmins now made their come-back by incorporating virtually all the innovations into a new synthesis of an all-embracing and multilevel system. This included not only the high spiritual teachings, but also the substream of popular and even tribal cults. The new synthesis thus allowed the simpler worshipper and the sophisticated thinker alike to choose their own medium of approach to the divine or to the realization of the final goal.

Renunciation, so important in the unorthodox movements, was not the way favoured by community-minded brahmins and so it was accommodated towards the end of the newly elaborated scheme of stages of life. But it was tolerated in those whose strong commitment led them to become *saṁnyāsis* while still young, and eventually even Hindu monastic orders developed. Yoga was also incorporated and given a prominent place in its classical form codified by Patañjali and it was even popularized and utilized for the renewal of the attitude of allegiance to a personal God. This led to the development of the *bhakti* trends in yoga. The Bhagavad Gītā even adapted the yoga path to the active life, reconciling its goal with the fulfilment of one's duties to society; it came to be known as Karma Yoga.

The process of this renewal and enlargement of the sphere of Vedic-Brahmanic tradition was greatly helped also by the reversion to it of patronage by the majority of royal dynasties in post-Mauryan times. The tradition was, however, greatly changed so that from then on it truly deserves a new name, and 'Hinduism' fits the bill very well, although the word was coined much later.

8. **The growth of medieval Hinduism**. The tendencies towards recognizing one God as *the* Lord which made themselves felt in some post-Buddhist Upaniṣads such as the Śvetāśvatara and also in the Bhagavad Gītā did not prevail in the all-embracing climate of Hindu revivalism, which allowed scores of local deities into the system. The problem led to the

development of the notion of *iṣṭa devatā*, which also enabled the accommodation of strong sectarian allegiances to newly elevated gods such as Viṣṇu, Śiva or the Devī. Eventually the Brahminic theologians developed the doctrine of the divine trinity (Trimūrti) with an enhanced role for the chief gods' divine spouses.

Another important feature of the new outlook was the belief in divine incarnations, first fully spelled out in the Bhagavad Gita, and elaborated into a systematic doctrine especially in the context of the cult of Viṣṇu. Religious topics and ethical principles are worked into the fabric of the national epical narratives of the Rāmāyaṇa and Mahābhārata, which were known to everybody. Further influence on the multitudes was exercised by the mythological and legendary stories of the Purāṇas which reworked materials from ancient Vedic tradition and from local, and even some tribal, religious cults, and presented newly developed Hindu mainstream teachings and sectarian theological speculations in a popular form. Ritual, much more simple and affordable than during the past peak of Brahminic domination, regained its importance and so did periodic religious festivals. Temple worship of gods developed and pilgrimages to famous shrines, temples and other sacred places connected with mythical and legendary events became an important feature of religious life.

9. **The development of schools of Hindu philosophy**. Philosophical inquiry in the sense of conceptual, rather than metaphorical and symbolical, formulations of questions and answers about the nature of existence and its meaning, including human destiny, can already be traced in the Ṛg Veda, the best example being the so-called Creation hymn 10,129, and reached its early peak in some Upaniṣadic passages. In the subsequent competition with rival movements such as Jainism and Buddhism the adherents of the Vedic-Brahminic tradition, enriched in their outlook by the accommodation of new trends, developed their teachings into systematically presented sets of tenets which they supported by rational arguments and often also by reference to special means of direct knowledge available to those trained in yoga.

These tenets were also, in their argumentation, sanctioned by revelation.

Six systems of 'orthodox' Hindu philosophy were eventually recognized: Yoga (codified by Patañjali), Sāṅkhya, Vaiśeṣika, Nyāya, Pūrva Mīmāṁsā and Utara Mīmāṁsā (Vedānta), some of them further split into sub-schools, differing among themselves in some details as to the interpretation of reality and of the relevant texts of the Vedic revelation. These schools cover, in their own way, virtually the whole field of human knowledge, but despite their many differences over some points, they are not regarded as mutually exclusive, because in the relative world of human learning the absolute truth cannot be presented fully and adequately and each particular system approaches it from a different vantage point which has its justification.

Along with this specialized development of philosophical thought there was another line of philosophising going on, on a much more popular level, which made the basic teachings of Hinduism, common to all its sections, widely known. These basic teachings eventually came to be epitomized by the concept of Sanātana Dharma, which has, of course, its popular as well as sophisticated versions.

10. **Neo-Hinduism or modern developments in Hinduism**. The sudden encounter of Hinduism with Western civilization brought into it some new perspectives and initiated in it also a process of re-assessment of itself. Previous confrontations with Islam had made little impact on it, and the only serious attempt at reconciliation or synthesis of the two traditions ended in the birth of a new faith, namely Sikhism. Christianity seemed to pose a certain threat, because it shared, to a degree, in the political prestige of the new rulers, and one of the reactions to it was the movement of Ārya Samāj with its drive to return 'back to the Vedas'. Another influence which came, however, from the fringe of the Christian scene led to the birth of Brahmo Samāj, a reformist Unitarian movement which was in fact influenced even more by the liberal ideas of the West than by its religion, as was even Ārya Samāj, although to a lesser

extent, and without readily admitting it. Western liberal ideas helped in the effort of the reformists to cleanse Hinduism of some negative developments, such as the excesses of the caste system or child marriage.

One Western idea, quite new to the Hindu way of thinking, had, at least initially, a rather strong impact, namely evolution. It was combined with the Hindu world view by Theosophists and found some echo in the teachings of one or two modern *gurus*, e.g. Aurobindo, but in the end it did not change the overall Hindu perspective of repetitive rounds of *saṁsāra* which does not admit of a final state of perfection to be reached through the steady progress of evolution.

If there is, however, one single idea which was prompted and gained prominence within Hinduism in the course of the encounters with the West, it is *universalism*. Foundations for it were already laid when the feature of Hinduism as being all-inclusive and capable of accommodating a variety of perspectives of the divine and the ways to it was accepted at the time when Hinduism was born as a new synthesis. It was further highlighted for a few, although with limited impact, by the perception of Kabīr. But enhanced by the dissemination of European ideas through education which led to the widening of intellectual horizons, universalism came to be absorbed into Hinduism as its own consciously adopted stance and outlook in opposition to Christianity's claim to be the sole vehicle of salvation and against the pretences of some modern secular ideologies. While recognizing the role of other religions and even their capacity to guide their followers to salvation, Hinduism came to perceive itself as more or less a universal religion into which other religions neatly fit, much as do the many diverse sectarian developments within it, whether those religions are able to recognize it or not.

This stance or an attitude similar to it can be seen as present implicitly or explicitly in quite a number of recent developments, e.g. in the life and teaching of Ramakrishna and in the work of the Ramakrishna Mission, in the activities of Gāndhī, in the works of Aurobindo as well as Radhakrishnan and even in the speeches of Krishnamurti,

> although he himself would never have agreed with the view that he belonged to Hindu tradition and carefully avoided Hindu terminology, while in fact representing one of the high peaks in the universalistic aspirations of modern Hinduism. On the orthodox scene modern developments have almost removed the limitations which previously led to exclusion from the fold of Hindus who travelled overseas and which prevented acceptance into the fold of those who were not born Hindus.

While realization of the universalistic nature, and perhaps even mission, of Hinduism on the religious scene of the world may have been prompted by its encounter with European civilization, its overall world view as expressed by the concept of Sanātana Dharma is nothing if not universal in outlook. It presents a picture of the universe which is multidimensional, hierarchical, in a way everlasting, and governed by an inherent universal law which finds expression in all its concrete manifestations.

Broadly speaking, a Hindu believes in an ever-revolving round of existence which conjures up a sequence of world manifestations and world withdrawals. When the universe is in its stage of manifestation, it has a multitude of structured existential dimensions, from places of deepest suffering to abodes of almost unimaginable bliss. These dimensions are inhabited by a variety of beings who are born in their respective situations according to their merits and the stage of their mental development. They range from subhuman modes of being of demon-like and animal life to superhuman and god-like forms of existence, differing from each other not in their innermost essence, but only in their characters and outward appearances, both of them acquired in the course of successive lives as a result of their actions, desires, uncontrolled or controlled urges, efforts, decisions and aspirations, or the lack of them. This is how the universal law works in the lives of individual beings, termed in this context the law of *karma*. When they eventually develop in themselves a capacity for self-observation and reflection, so that they begin to comprehend their situation, they reach thereby a position in which they can make a decision to turn inwards to realize their true inner essence and thereby to avoid for themselves the necessity of going through a seemingly endless round of limited forms of existence. This is liberation or salvation, i.e. *mokṣa*. Such is the overall picture expressed by the concept of Sanātana Dharma.

Against this background of a lofty world view, ordinary life of course goes on and the average Hindu busies himself with the immediate affairs of his life and enlists all the help he can get from his tradition, on the level on which he can grasp it, in order to steer those affairs in the desired direction. Much of what he understands of his tradition may be far removed from the ideal picture outlined above. Distorted interpretations of his tradition, social prejudice perceived as sacred heritage, and misconceived ideas about the working of karmic laws are often the background for his decisions and ways of behaviour. The desire to emulate a Western life-style often leads to the adoption of its negative features, which weaken the hold of Hindu spiritual values over him. Political, economic, social, communal and nationalistic issues may also divert him away from true spirituality. Nevertheless the opportunity to make use of the profound message of Hinduism and to shape his life accordingly is always there, even if the start and the pace of progress may, with many, be modest and on a rather superficial level.

Two points still deserve special mention, although a thoughtful reader will have become aware of them from what has already been discussed. They should always be borne in mind by anyone watching Hindu customs and practices or evaluating the beliefs and behaviour of Hindus. The first point is the multi-level nature of Hinduism, which allows for every and any form of approach to the transcendent, from worship in front of a peculiarly shaped stone or at the foot of a sacred tree to elaborate rituals in temples; from constant repetition of a name of God to articulate prayer, singing of mantras or wordless meditation in deep absorption; from the frenzied emotion of a *bhakta* to the cool conceptual analysis of a philosopher or the measured progressive training for the sake of developing sharp insight by a practitioner of Jñāna Yoga. At the same time one should not regard one approach as higher, more efficient or more appropriate than another. Each of them may prove itself capable of leading the respective practitioner to the very threshold of the mystery of the transcendent, from where he either does or does not take the final leap, according to his volition and on the basis of his own understanding.

It is not for the observer to pass judgment on the intrinsic value of the various approaches for a genuine chance of the final realization by the practitioner, except that he may perhaps be justified in trying to assess the practitioner's sincerity and degree of involvement.

If this first point is not borne in mind, and its validity accepted, misunderstandings and misjudgements can easily occur. They occurred in the past with academic indologists who did not have a full overview of Hinduism and were as yet unaware of the multidimensionality of its symbols, rituals and scriptural messages, and also with Christian missionaries, anthropological researchers or short-term visitors, each with his particular stance and a preconceived objective, and therefore with limited capacity, and sometimes unwillingness, to take in the subtler meanings behind gross phenomena.

The second point to bear in mind concerns the possible limited vision and understanding of the insider. Some Hindus are trapped in a kind of capsule within the vast system of Hinduism. It may be determined by their sectarian allegiance, their caste origin, their status in the community, their traditionalism, the views or teachings of their *guru* and their various vested interests. In the absence of a central authority, which Hinduism has never had, to decide on controversial issues, there are bound to be conflicting reactions to them, interpretations will differ and so will ways of solving problems. Thus the limited vision of some prevents them from accepting Western members of the Hare Krishna movement as genuine Hindus and some even deny the whole movement its place within the Hindu tradition, on the grounds of its world-wide orientation. Yet others show their customary respect to a *sādhu* roaming the Indian plains even if he happens to be a Westerner. Gāndhī dedicated much effort to raising the status of the lowest, officially designated as 'scheduled', classes of Hindu society, the 'untouchables', calling them Harijans, the children of God. In contrast to this, a few years ago high caste Hindu youngsters in Bihār set themselves on fire in protest against a governmental scheme to improve Harijans' prospects of obtaining higher occupations. And there are many other such dichotomies.

Yet there is always a solution for those who seek it, which is, paradoxically, only individual, although it has universal validity. The highest authority in Hinduism is Sanātana Dharma with its global vision of the world and its anticipation of the goal of life: liberation. From this universalistic vantage point all concrete issues can be approached with a good chance of adequate solution according to the circumstances, but it will always depend on the right perception of the individual or on his willingness to work it out for himself. In a way this is also true for the outsider – for a certain type of academic, for the tourist or for the visitor on business who gets a glimpse of the bewildering variety of the Hindu religious scene. It is further true, no doubt, for the Westerner in his home, who is confronted with unfamiliar customs in the life of his immigrant neighbours. And so it is hoped that this Dictionary may help towards an overview and deeper understanding of Hinduism for all those who may need it and can benefit from it.

Compiling this Dictionary has inevitably involved a process of selection in sifting through an enormous number of possible entries. In some areas, such as mythology, the omissions had to be drastic and readers seeking further information should resort to a specialized or popular work in Indian mythology or to a larger encyclopedia of Hinduism.[1] Similar limitations in the number of entries had to be accepted also with respect to leading personages in the context of sectarian developments, schools of philosophy, monasteries, missions and *āśrams*, both historical and modern.[2] Most users are likely to have read some basic book

[1] For example:

Dowson, John, *A Classical Dictionary of Hindu Mythology and Religion, Geography, History, and Literature*, 9th edn., Routledge & Kegan Paul, London, 1957.

Garg, Ganda Ram (general editor), *Encyclopaedia of the Hindu World*, Concept Publishing Company, New Delhi, 1992. (An on-going project, still dealing with the letter A.)

Stutley, Margaret & James, *A Dictionary of Hinduism, its Mythology, Folklore and Development 1500 B.C.–A.D. 1500*, Routledge & Kegan Paul, London and Henley, 1977.

Walker, Benjamin: *Hindu World. An Encyclopedic Survey of Hinduism*, 2 vols., George Allen & Unwin, London, 1968.

[2] For a comprehensive book on Hinduism which is packed with information, sometimes going into considerable detail, see:

Brockington, J. L., *The Sacred Thread. Hinduism in its Continuity and Diversity*, Edinburgh University Press, 1981.

on the subject they are interested in and this Dictionary should enable them to put it into a wider context within Hinduism.

A limited number of English terms or concepts important for the understanding of Hinduism have been included, e.g. 'Absolute', 'Cosmogony', 'Caste', 'Liberation', 'Marriage', 'Transmigration' etc. Reading them and the cross-references where given, while browsing through the Dictionary, may provide for a 'beginner' who knows very little about Hinduism an initial picture of its basic tenets and its more conspicuous features.

*Oṁ śānti!*

A number of books giving an overview of Hinduism is available. There is, however, a lack of truly comprehensive and detailed works on Hinduism in English. Further information has to be sought in specialized monographs.

**a** the first letter of the Sanskrit alphabet; the first component of *praṇava*, the most sacred *mantra oṁ* (*a-u-ṁ*); the symbol of creation; a name of Viṣṇu (Aḥ).

**Ābhāsvaras** ('the lustrous ones') gods of a higher spiritual realm; a group of sixty-four deities in Śiva's retinue.

***abhaya*** fearlessness. Freedom from fear is a state acquired in full only in liberation.

***abhaya mudrā*** the gesture of fearlessness, known in particular from images of the Buddha, is in Hinduism characteristic of Viṣṇu.

***abheda*** non-difference, an Advaitic term which describes the world as identical with *brahman*, the only true reality.

**Abhinava Gupta** (tenth century A.D.) a writer on aesthetics and a philosopher of the Kashmiri school of Śaivism who wrote over forty works.

***abhiṣeka*** consecration by sprinkling with holy water; an initiation, inauguration, coronation or installation ceremony.

**Absolute** a philosophical term by which is meant the ultimate and unconditioned transcendental reality, regarded in Hinduism also as the source of phenomenal reality, i.e. of the created universe, and termed usually *brahman*. It is central to Hindu philosophy and while it is admitted to be beyond conceptual grasp, it is always understood to possess the highest intrinsic intelligence, as is clearly expressed in one of the 'Great Sayings' (*mahāvākyas*): *prajñānam brahma*, i.e. *brahman* is intelligence (or wisdom – AU 3,3), and it is sometimes referred to in terms of personality, albeit an infinite one, for which there is a precedence already in the hymn of the RV on the cosmic Person (*puruṣa*, 10,90). In other hymns of the RV it is called *aja*, the unborn (1,164,6; 8,41,10; 10,16,4; 10,82,6), and *tad ekam*, 'that one', in the Creation hymn (10,129). It is also expressed in mythological ways, e.g. by the figure of the goddess Aditi who gave birth to the world, etc. The AV is the first to use the term *brahman* a few times (e.g. 11,8,32) in the sense of the Absolute in which it was later firmly established in the Upaniṣads. It designates the Absolute in Vedāntic systems also. It is further used in mainstream Hinduism which, however, occasionally employs various other terms as well. Sectarian teachings usually regard their highest God as possessing both the status of the impersonal Absolute, i.e. *brahman*, and the highest personhood, and prefer to relate to the Absolute in terms of their personal God or Lord (*īśvara*).

**Absorption** a term used in connection with the states of consciousness developed in the course of mind training for the purpose of spiritual progress, particularly through the techniques of yoga. Its Skt. equivalent may differ with the textual context, but the most frequent terms would be *dhyāna* and *samādhi* qualified by attributes according to the nature or degree of the state of absorption.

**Abu**, also: Abū, Arbuda, Arbada (=serpent) a mountain in West Rājasthān sacred to the followers of Śiva and Viṣṇu as well as to Jains. Rājpūts from the clan known by the name Agnikūla derive their descent from the sacred fire on Mount Abu.

***ācārya*** teacher, preceptor; spiritual guide or leader within a particular tradition or sect.

***acintya*** unthinkable, incomprehensible, inexplicable; an attribute of the Divine Absolute, sometimes used as its name (Acintya).

**Acintya Bhedābheda** a school of Vedānta which teaches that the individual is both different and non-different from *brahman* or God, a conception which is rationally inexplicable, but realizable by *bhakti* practice. Cf. Nimbārka and Bhedābheda.

***acit*** unconscious; this is Rāmānuja's term for matter which, as the material universe, forms the body of God.

**Action** (*karma*), and not divine providence or will, is the force which determines all events both in an individual's life and in the world at large, according to the underlying philosophy of Hinduism. It operates on three levels, in thought, in speech and in actual deeds, Human life as well as the progress and decline of civilizations is the result of individual and collective tendencies, drives and decisions prevailing in the minds of people and consciously taken and acted upon.

**Adam's bridge**, also: Rāma's bridge the name for the chain of islets and sandbanks (*setubandha*) between the islands of Rāmeśvaram off the southern tip of India and Mannar off the north coast of Sri Lanka which could be crossed on foot till 1480 when a storm breached it. According to the epic Rāmāyaṇa it was built by Hanumān's forces helping Rāma to cross over to Rāvaṇa's kingdom in Laṅkā in order to recover the abducted Sītā. The Islamic tradition maintains that after the expulsion from paradise Adam crossed by this way to Ceylon (Sri Lanka).

***adarśana*** ignorance; inability to see truth.

***adharma*** lawlessness; state of 'fall' into phenomenality; lack of righteousness or integrity; moral and spiritual decadence.

***ādhibhautika*** concerned with material forces or elements; material; worldly; phenomenal; one of the three levels of interpretation of the Vedas according to Yāska's *Nirukta*, namely the lowest one.

***ādhidaivika*** concerned with deities; theological; the second of the three levels of interpretation of the Vedas according to Yāska's *Nirukta*.

***adhika māsa*** the thirteenth, intercalary, lunar month inserted in the Hindu calendar after every thirty lunar months to make up for the approximately eleven day difference between the lunar and solar years. It is also called *mala māsa* (impure month) during which some rites, such as marriage, should not take place, and those who have neglected their religious duties or vows should make up for it by increased effort and practice.

***adhvaryu*** the YV brahmin; the officiating priest who builds the altar, prepares sacrificial vessels and fires and performs the animal sacrifice, while chanting appropriate texts from the YV, under the guidance of the *hotar*.

***adhyāsa*** superimposition; false attribution (as in the mistaken perception of a snake instead of a rope in semi-darkness). It is an Advaitic philosophical term trying to explain away the reality of the world as illusion veiling the only true reality, namely *brahman*, and caused by ignorance.

***adhyātman*** overself; supreme spirit; absolute reality.

***ādhyātmika*** pertaining to the self or to the essence of reality; essential; spiritual; absolute, nouminal; the highest of the three levels of interpretation of the Vedas according to Yāska's *Nirukta*.

***ādi*** beginning; original, primeval, archetypal.

**Ādi Buddha** the personalized form of the transcendental principle of enlightenment in Mahāyāna and Tantric Buddhism.

**Ādi Granth** (also: Granth Sāhib) the sacred book of the Sikhs installed in the Golden Temple of Amritsar (since 1604).

**Ādinātha** 'Primal Lord'. In Jainism: the designation of the first *tīrthaṅkara*. In the Nātha cult: Śiva as the Supreme Siddha and the first teacher of Yoga as a path to perfection.

**Ādi-Purāṇa** usually the Brahma Purāṇa is meant.

**ādi-śakti** the primordial energy of the universe, a Śaktic term for the original state of *prakṛti* represented in a personalized form by the Goddess, usually as Kālī.

**Ādi-Śaṅkara** Śaṅkara as the main representative and the first *ācārya* of the Advaita Vedānta school of philosophy, so called to distinguish him from his successors who bear his name as a title.

**Aditi** (infinity) one of the most ancient Vedic gods, representing the boundlessness of the transcendent Absolute. She is described as the mother of men, gods and all creatures (RV 1,86,10. AV 7,61), the protectress and guide of those who have made spiritual vows and the queen of the eternal law (AV 7,6,2; VS 21,5). Later she was identified with 'Mother Earth' and the 'Cosmic Cow', but her actual appearance was never described. The only part of her that was ever referred to was her womb, out of which the world was born. She was the centre of one of the oldest creation myths of the Vedas, representing the original infinite dimension of the unmanifest before the world (her offspring) came into being and indicating by her nature as goddess that reality in its pre-manifest latency is not the mere precreational chaos of philosophers (or the subatomic plasma of astrophysicists heading for a 'big bang'), but an intelligent and infinite divine personage: in her bringing forth the world and giving birth to beings there is an intelligent design. Her first offspring were the Ādityas, one of them being Dakṣa, and Aditi then became his daughter. Thus she herself was born into the manifested world as a deity so that her role within subsequent mythical world history is in this secondary guise. This may be the first ever recorded indication of the doctrine of divine incarnations.

**Āditya** the son of Aditi, usually referring to the Sun as deity; in pl. Ādityas are a group of six, seven or eight gods, the foremost sons of Aditi. The lists vary, but those most often named are: Varuṇa, Mitra, Āryaman, Bhaga, Dakṣa, Aṁśa. Others some times named are: Dhātar, Indra, Vivasvat or Sūrya and Mārtaṇḍa. In post-Vedic times their number was increased to twelve and they were associated with months of the year.

***advaita*** non-dual.

**Advaita Vedānta** non-dual or monistic view of reality derived from the Upaniṣads and elaborated into a system of philosophy whose best known representative is Śaṅkara. The Upaniṣadic teaching about the identity of the universal and the individual, i.e. of the source of reality as a whole and the essence of individual beings and things (which is expressed in the Upaniṣads by the equation *brahman*=*ātman*), is interpreted by this school in the sense which proclaims *brahman* to be the sole and only reality besides which nothing else really exists. The manifested universe (including individual beings) is illusory and unreal and comes about by a false limitation imposed on *brahman* by the mind's ignorance, just as the illusory ideal of 'snake' may be imposed on a rope by the mind ignorant of its true nature when seeing it in semi-darkness (cf. *adhyāsa* – superimposition). Since the mind itself is unreal and an imposition on *brahman*, the sole and only true reality, it is again *brahman* who is responsible for it all. The vexed question of the reason or motivation for producing the whole gigantic spectacle of the manifested universe with its multiplicity of ignorant minds is never fully tackled, except by suggesting that it is a divine game or sport (cf. *līlā*).

**Adyār** originally a town east of Madrās, now its suburb, the seat of the headquarters of the Theosophical Society.

***ādya-śrādha*** a substitute funerary rite which can be performed during one's lifetime. It is meant for those Hindus who have no son to conduct funerary rites for them or for some reason believe that they will not be performed for them after their death.

***āgama*** arrival, acquisition, accumulation.

**Āgamas** sectarian works which contain mythological, epical and philosophical materials, alternative or supplementary to traditional scriptures. They are usually regarded by their respective sectarian followers as the 'fifth Veda' and therefore as divine revelation. Only Śaiva Āgamas always retain the word in their titles, the Vaiṣṇava sectarian scriptures are usually called Saṁhitās and the Śākta sources are mostly called Tantras.

***agni*** fire; one of the four elements (earth, water, air, fire, with space or ether sometimes added as the fifth) or physical forces constituting the material universe.

**Agni** god of fire, especially of the sacrificial fire. He is the priest of the gods and the mediator between gods and their human worshippers.

***agnicayana*** the ceremonial act of preparing the *vedi*, i.e. the altar or the fireplace for a sacrifice.

***agnihotra*** a fire offering; a daily Vedic household rite whose offering consists mostly of milk, oil and sour gruel.

**Agnikūla** a division of Rājpūts who derive their descent from Agni on Mount Abu (as distinct from those who claim Lunar or Solar origins). The legend may have originated in the Brahminic fire ceremony by which invading warriors who settled in the country and became rulers of parts of it were elevated to the *kṡatriya* status and thereby legitimized.

***agniṣṭoma*** the offering of *soma*, an important and complicated Vedic rite which usually lasted five days.

***aham brahmāsmi*** 'I am *brahman*' (BU 1,4,10), one of several pronouncements from the early Upaniṣads which later came to be called the 'Great Sayings' (*mahāvākyas*). It expresses the Vedāntic philosophy of the essential oneness between the individual and the Divine source of reality and probably stemmed originally from the overwhelming inner experience of the Upanisadic sages when they discovered in meditational absorptions (*dhyāna*) that their true 'I' was not the superficial *ego* of everyday life, but their innermost self (*ātman*), and that on that deep level they were at one with God. The idea that God dwells deep down in the heart of everybody came to be a widely held tenet even among the simplest followers of Hinduism.

***ahaṅkāra*** 'I-maker', 'I-am-ness'; egoity; the principle of individuality. In some systems of philosophy it is regarded as a cosmic force, e.g. in Sāṅkhya it is the first cosmic evolute from the Mahat or the cosmic *buddhi* and a state of manifestation of the universe characterized by the separative tendency of *guṇas*, the three dynamic forces of *prakṛti*.

**Ahi** 'serpent', another Vedic name for Vṛtra, the dragon or demon of darkness and inertia (and precreational 'chaos'). It is applied also to the demon Rāhu, periodically swallowing the moon, and to monsoon clouds, holding waters which are released by Indra's spear (=lightning).

***ahiṁsā*** non-injury, harmlessness; abstaining from evil towards others in deed, word and thought. Propagated by radical early renouncers outside the Vedic tradition, it became a part of the ethics and practice of Jainism, Buddhism and classical Yoga (as the first *yama* of Patañjali's *aṣṭaṅga yoga*) and later influenced a large part of Hinduism, leading to wide-spread adoption of vegetarianism and virtual abandonment of animal sacrifices.

**Ahirbudhnya** 'the serpent of the depths', another Vedic name for Vṛtra as the precreational cosmic dimension of latency; later also an epithet of Śiva as the Absolute.

**Airāvata, Airāvaṇa** a white elephant with four tusks, one of the products of the churning of the celestial ocean. Indra adopted him as his mount and rides him when causing rain so that he has become associated with clouds.

***aja*** 'unborn', the Vedic expression for the transcendent or hidden force supporting reality, later known as *brahman/ātman*; goat; sacrificial goat which was tied to a sacrificial pole before the ritual of sacrifice started.

**Ajā** (f., the unborn one) another name for Māya; *ajā-śakti*: the unborn energy (another name for *ādi-śakti*) said in Śaktic mythology (which emulates Purāṇic Trimurti) to have assumed three forms, namely Mahāsarasvatī (representing creation), Mahālakṣmī (preservation) and Mahākālī (destruction).

**Aja Ekapād** ('one-legged goat') a Vedic god often called the 'supporter of the sky'. He combines in himself the associations that go with the sacrificial pole, Indra's spear, the axis of the world, the creation of the universe, and the double meaning of the word *aja* as the unborn source of the world and a sacrificial animal. He thus appears to symbolize the process of creation as a cosmic sacrifice out of the transcendental force itself, the infinite, yet person-like, unborn Absolute (cf. *puruṣa*), which even after the creation is supporting the manifested universe and is therefore its permanent prop. This is reminiscent of Indra's spear propping up heaven after he separated heaven and earth and it points to a further association of the image with the *axis mundi* which goes right through the whole of creation as a connecting route between heaven and earth, i.e. the transcendental dimension and the phenomenal world.

**Ajantā** a famous site near Aurangabad with Buddhist cave shrines and temples dated from the second century B.C. till the seventh century A.D. It is important also for the iconography of Hindu deities.

**Ajita Keśakambali** (cca 500 B.C.) a *nāstika* and *lokāyata*, i.e. an antireligious and materialist philosopher who believed that everything was just a combination of the four material elements (earth, water, air, fire), and that individual beings ceased to exist after death.

**Ajīvika** a *nāstika* (i.e. denying the validity of the Vedic tradition) and deterministic school of thought which probably already existed around 700 B.C. and was prominent around 500 B.C. It contained the teaching of four elements, the atomic theory and the view that all events, including the fate of beings in successive lives, were the result of destiny (*niyati*) and that everybody would reach an end of sorrow at the appointed time after a certain fixed number of world periods.

***ājñā*** (command) ***cakra*** the spiritual centre in the subtle body, located between the eyebrows. It is in the shape of a lotus with two petals, as taught in the Kuṇḍalinī Yoga system.

***akāla*** timeless, an epithet of *brahman*.

**Akāla** a name of Brahma.

***ākāśa*** space, ether; sometimes added as fifth to the four 'great elements' (earth, water, air, fire) which form material reality.

***akṣara*** imperishable; letter 'a'; Oṁ as the imperishable sound; a designation for *brahman*.

**Akṣarā** a name of goddess Vāc.

**Alakṣmī** the goddess of misfortune, the older sister of Lakṣmī.

**Allāhābād (Ilāhābād)** see Prayāga.

**Almsgiving** is very important in Hinduism as a source of acquiring merit for future lives on the one hand, and as a means of support for ascetics, mendicants and *sādhus* of many varieties who live only on charity, on the other. The saintlier the recipient, the greater the merit derived from giving.

**Āḻvār** (Tamil: 'lost in God') a designation for the Tamil Vaiṣṇava poets and saints (active mainly from the seventh to the tenth century A.D.), leaders of South Indian Vaiṣṇava devotional movements, often authors of devotional hymns praising Nārāyaṇa, Rāma and the love games of Kṛṣṇa. They were also singers and musicians and opposed the orthodox Brahminic monopolism of worship and the caste system.

**Amarāvatī** ('place of immortality') the name of Indra's celestial abode; a medieval city on the river Kistna in Andhra Pradesh, once a centre of Buddhist learning (now a village, but with a state College).

**Aṁbā** (vern. 'mother'), also: Aṁbā Bhavānī a name of Durgā.

**Ambedkar, Bhīmrāo Rām** (1891–1956) leader of the untouchables, who fought for their emancipation by legal means. As the son of an army school headmaster, he received a good early education. Supported by the Mahārāja of Baroda, he obtained a grant and was the first untouchable to be awarded a B.A. degree in Bombay in 1912, then in Columbia an M.A. in 1915 and a Ph.D. in 1916. Later he studied law at Gray's Inn and Political Science in the London School of Economics, before entering politics back home. He was the first Law Minister (1947–51) in independent India and drafted its Constitution, which outlawed castes and untouchability. As his efforts to raise the actual status of his fellow untouchables in Hindu society made little headway because of widespread Hindu prejudice, he saw no place for them or himself within Hinduism and publicly embraced Buddhism in October 1956. Many mass conversions of untouchables took place subsequently. He died suddenly on 6th December of the same year.

**Aṁbikā** one of the names or incarnations of Umā, the wife of Śiva (popular also with Jains). Her name occurs first in the VS, but there she is Rudra's sister. Originally perhaps a nature goddess, she is still associated with autumn.

***amṛta*** immortality; nectar, the drink of immortality which, according to a Purāṇic myth, was obtained by the gods and demons (*asuras*), who were originally mortal, when churning the cosmic ocean. According to one mythological version it is stored in the moon, which periodically refills after the gods and blessed ancestors have drunk the nectar from it, thus accounting for its waning and waxing.

***aṁśa*** partial incarnation of god.

**Aṁśa** one of the Ādityas, representing the quality of sharing, apportioning, evaluating.

***anādi*** (without beginning) eternal, an epithet of *brahman* and Brahmā or of the highest deity.

***anāhata*** 'unstruck', i.e. silent; *anāhata cakra*: the spiritual centre in the subtle body opposite the central point of the chest, in the shape of a twelve-petalled lotus; *anāhata śabda*: the mystic sound *oṁ* heard in the *cakra* when reached by Kuṇḍalinī in her upward movement.

***ānanda*** bliss; the third component of the compound *saccidānanda*, designating the experience of the ultimate reality in the Advaita Vedānta system; *ānanda tāṇḍava*: an ecstatic dance of joy.

***ānandamaya*** 'consisting of bliss', 'bliss-like'; *ānandamaya kośa* ('bliss-made sheath'): a Vedāntic term for the highest or spiritual body in the system of five sheaths, the other four *kośas* being: *annamaya*, *prāṇamaya*, *manomaya*, and *vijñānamaya*.

**Ānandamayī Mā** (1896–1982) a modern Hindu spiritual teacher and mystic. Born in the village of Kheora, now in Bangladesh, she spent most of her life wandering, later between many *āśrams* founded by her for her followers. Her teaching can be described as a kind of ecstatic *bhakti* with Advaitic background combined with a certain tolerance or respect for traditional Hindu observances, but the goal is the realisation of oneness.

**Ānand Mārg** a neo-Hindu movement with predominantly social and educational aims. Founded in 1955 at Jamālpur by Prahbāt Ranjan Sarkār, it spread throughout South and South East Asia and into the U.S.A., but less into Europe. Its headquarters, called Ānand Nagar, are in West Bengal. When it was suffering internal power struggles in the early seventies, a temporary ban was put on its activities in the U.S.A.

**Ananta** (infinite) the name of the cosmic snake (a symbol of never-ending cyclic time) on which Viṣṇu reclines in the icon based on Purāṇic mythology. His other name is Śeṣa or Ādiśeṣa and also Vāsuki.

***aneka*** ('not one') manifold.

**Aneka Liṅga** the manifold *liṅga* shrine, i.e. with a number of *liṅgas*, usually of the simple conical shape, but frequently of a large size. It is often found in South Indian Śivaistic temples.

**Aneka Mūrti** ('of many forms') a name of Viṣṇu.

***aṅga*** limb; part; auxiliary treatise.

**Aṅgiras** a legendary Vedic *ṛṣi* of divine status, father of Agni, associated with the AV which is sometimes called by his name.

**Angkor Vat** (or Wat; lit. 'city temple') a monumental Khmer temple complex in present-day Cambodia (Kampuchea; orig. Khmer: Kambuja) built by king Sūryavarman II (1112–52) in the shape of the Hindu model of the universe with its central tower representing Mount Meru. The galleries contain superb reliefs of scenes from BP (churning of the cosmic ocean), Mhb, and Rāmāyaṇa. Although the concept is Viṣṇuistic, the central tower is believed to have housed a *liṅga* representing the king's divinity as was the case with earlier Khmer hill top temples. It was replaced with a statue of the Buddha during the reign of Jayavaram VII (1181–1218) who built inside Angkor Thom, his capital, the Bayon temple with giant faces of the Bodhisattva Lokeśvara, believed to bear the features of the king himself.

***añjali*** a respectful obeisance to a superior by slightly bowing the head, placing one's palms together, with a cavity between them, and raising them towards one's forehead.

***anna*** food, sustenance; Annadevī: goddess of nourishment.

***annamaya kośa*** ('food-made sheath') a Vedāntic term for the physical body in the system of five sheaths, the other four *kośas* being: *prāṇamaya*, *manomaya*, *vijñānamaya* and *ānandamaya*.

**Annapūrṇā** the name of Durgā as the goddess of plenty.

***antaḥpura*** female apartments in a traditional Hindu household.

**Antaka** (the 'ender') a name of Yama, the king of the realm of the deceased ones and their judge.

**Āṇṭāḷ** (ninth century A.D.) a South Indian female *bhakti* poet said to have been married to Viṣṇu's statue at Śrīraṅgam and eventually absorbed into it. She is locally worshipped as an incarnation of Śrī.

***antarikṣa*** interim space; atmosphere; air; intermediary region (between the material and the spiritual world).

***antaryāmi*** 'inner controller', an Upaniṣadic expression for *brahman* immanent to all beings as *ātman*. The expression is later used also in monistic religious teachings to indicate the presence of God within (in the hearts of men). It became the basis for the later theory of *vyūha*.

***aṇu*** atom; in post-classical Hindu teachings also one of the many designations for the individual 'soul'.

**Anu Gītā** (the 'miniature' Gītā) a recapitulation of the teachings of the BhG in the Mhb. It was given by Kṛṣṇa to Arjuna after the great war.

**Apabhraṁśa** the summary name for Indian dialects from about the seventh century A.D., following the period of medieval

Prākrits and preceding the period of modern Indian languages. Some Jain and Tantric works were written in various forms of it.

**Apām Napāt** ('son of the waters') a Vedic deity manifested in the lightning which issues from rain clouds.

***aparigraha*** non-grasping, non-acquisitiveness, one of the *yamas* in Patañajali's *aṣṭaṅga yoga*.

**Āpas ('waters')** lower deities described in the RV as maidens (symbolical of the cosmic potential of world manifestation) and young wives and mothers (symbolical of the creative forces of manifestation). Broadly speaking, terms like 'cosmic waters', 'cosmic ocean', 'world ocean' are used in various contexts for the unmanifest reality before the world came into existence. The symbolism of waters indicates that they harbour the virtually infinite multiplicity of things and beings which appear in the world after its manifestation. They further symbolize the (cosmic) mind or the 'element of mentality', most of which is unconscious and harbours various drives and seeds of potential qualities and capabilities not yet revealed or realized. As a cosmic element, waters are associated with the moon, which also sometimes stands for the mind and especially for its unconscious part.

**Apasmāra** the name of the demon-dwarf, symbolical of ignorance, who is being stamped on by Śiva Naṭarāja.

***apauruṣeya*** 'not of human origin', an epithet of the Veda, expressing the belief that it is a divine revelation and is of superhuman origin.

***apsaras*** heavenly nymph; a category of lower female deities (originally probably aquatic nymphs) who wait on gods and beings reborn in Indra's heaven, delighting them with song and dance (their male counterparts: *gandharvas*). Sometimes *apsarases* befriend men on earth and give birth to their children. At the request of Indra they occasionally contrive to seduce ascetics who have become too powerful for his comfort. They also conduct heroes fallen in battle to Indra's heaven (cf. the Valkyries of Germanic mythology).

***arahat, arhat, arahant*** ('the worthy one') a designation of ascetics as worthy of reverence and material support and hence regarded as advanced in spiritual achievement. It was adopted by Buddhism as a specific designation of a liberated or enlightened person and is used also in Jainism in a similar sense.

***araṇya*** uncultivated land; forest.

***āraṇya*** forest dweller; hermit.

**Āraṇyakas** 'forest books'; a category of Vedic literature (*śruti*), following the Brāhmaṇas and preceding the Upaniṣads. They deal mainly with the cosmic significance of the Vedic rituals, but contain also mythological and legendary materials.

**Arbuda** a serpent-demon slain by Indra, probably an equivalent or another form of Vṛtra.

**Ardhanārī, Ardhanārīśa, Ardhanarīśvara** the hermaphroditic form of Śiva as half-man and half-woman, symbolizing for his followers his transcendental wholeness in which opposites are integrated.

**Arjuna** ('white') the name of the third Pāndu prince in the Mhb, a son of Indra. Kṛṣṇa related to him the teachings of the BhG before the great war started on the battlefield Kurukṣetra when Arjuna hesitated to engage in the battle.

***artha*** purpose, goal, sake; means, wealth, achievement, success; in the broad sense: goal of life as embodied in the Hindu ethical system of four human aims (*puruṣārthas*) to be realized in the life of a person, namely (1) *dharma* (duty, morality, religious observances), (2) *artha* in the narrow sense (wealth, prosperity, reputation or fame), (3) *kāma* (sensory and aesthetic fulfilment) and (4) *mokṣa* (liberation, salvation).

**Arthaśāstra** a work ascribed to the brahmin Kautilya, the minister of Chandragupta Maurya (cca 323–297 B.C.), on political theory and practice, extolling law and order and centralized authority.

**ārtī** (vern.; Skt. *āratī)* ceremonial waving of a lamp (*āratrika*) in front of an effigy of god as an offering of light during a *pūjā*.

**Aruṇācala** a hill near Tiruvaṇṇamalai, South India. The place was made widely known because of Ramaṇa Mahārṣi who settled there. The *āśram* which grew up round him at the foot of the hill still exists as a centre propagating his teachings.

**ārya** noble; Ārya(n): the designation which the IE tribes, who invaded India in the second millennium B.C. creating the Vedic civilization, used for themselves and which was once so used also by other IE nations (cf. Iran and Eire). It is often used instead of the designation IE, sometimes, not quite appropriately, with racial meaning.

**Āryaman** (Av. Airyaman) one of the Ādityas, representing the quality of nobleness, hospitality, protection and generosity.

**Ārya Samāj** a Hindu reform movement founded in 1875 by Dayānanda (1824–83) with the motto 'Back to the Vedas', but under the influence of some liberal modern ideas, resulting from European type education introduced to India. Although respecting caste distinctions, Dayānanda denied their religious status and introduced the 'rite of purification' (*śuddhi*) for readmission into Hinduism of converts to other religions. This developed into a wider *śuddhi* movement for low caste and outcast communities, giving them equal status with higher caste Hindus in religious matters, but it has not had a universal success, because of the resistance of high caste Hindus.

**Āryavarta** ('the land of the Āryans') the ancient name for North India between the two seas in the East and West and between the foothills of the Himālayas and the Vindhya ranges.

**āsana** seat, throne; sitting position for meditation; posture; bodily position or posture in the system of Hatha Yoga of which there are several dozens, with many variations; one of the *aṅgas* in Patañjali's *āṣṭaṅga yoga*, probably referring simply to a suitable sitting (cross-legged) position for meditation.

***asat*** non-being, non-existence; sometimes used in the sense of the latent state of reality prior to manifestation from which emerged *sat*, existence or phenomenal reality.

**Asceticism** (Skt. *tapas*) an important part of the Hindu religious scene, ranging from restraint of the senses, celibacy and general renunciation of worldly life, involving living on the bottom line of merely sustaining life, to the extremes of self-punishment and self-torture. Some measure of renunciation and control of the senses are regarded by most Indian religious movements as essential for spiritual progress on the path to liberation, while self-punishment is motivated by the belief, not generally shared, that it can atone for past karmic guilt and speed up liberation.

**Ashes** symbolically represent the pure substance left when phenomenal differentiating qualities have been removed. Being the result of a process which reduces multiplicity to unity, they also symbolize the path to liberation. They are used to make a mark on the forehead and some ascetics smear their whole body or powder their hair with ashes or take an 'ash bath'. They also have some use in Āyurvedic medicine.

***asteya*** non-stealing, one of the *yamas* in Patañjali's system of *aṣṭaṅga yoga*.

***āstika*** affirming (the validity of Vedic teachings and of the divine origin of the Vedas); orthodox.

**Astrology** (a part of the ancient lore of *jyotiṣa* which includes astronomy) is an important feature of Hinduism both for religious undertakings and in personal life, e.g. when selecting a marriage partner or deciding on dates of important events.

***asu*** (Vedic) breath, vitality, life-force.

***asura*** 'anti-god', demon, titan. In the oldest strata of the RV it was a designation for, or title of, high gods such as Varuṇa (cf. Av. Ahura Mazdā), because derived from *asu*, but this usage was later discarded when the Vedic gods lost much of their importance and the meaning of the term *asura* changed to denote the perpetual adversaries of *devas*, or 'anti-gods' (in part possibly as a result of the false etymology of the word as *a-sura* which led to the appearance of a new class of deities called *suras*).

***aśoka*** a tree sacred to Śiva, *Saraca indica*.

**Aśoka** (Pl. Asoka, cca 272–32 B.C.) the third and greatest king of the Maurya dynasty and the first emperor of India, who converted to Buddhism but supported all religious movements. He is famous for his rock edicts extolling charitable work, morality and piety in life.

***āśrama*** a stage of life; a hermitage or community home ('ashram') led by a *guru* or spiritual teacher. There are four stages of life in the ancient Brahminic scheme (referred to also as *āśrama dharma*); (1) *brahmacāri*, i.e. a student, disciple or apprentice, (2) *gṛhastha* or a householder, (3) *vānaprastha* or a forest dweller, and (4) *parivrājaka* or *saṅnyāsi*, which means a mendicant or homeless wanderer. These stages are largely only theoretical, because seldom followed by most Hindus.

***aśvamedha*** horse sacrifice, an elaborate rite which could be performed only by a powerful king who was able to ensure full protection to the sacrificial horse wherever it went while allowed to roam freely for a year, before the ritual sacrifice took place.

***aśvattha*** the pipal tree, *Ficus religiosa*.

**Aśvins** ('horse-riders'); also: Nāsatyas Vedic twin deities of IE origin (cf. Greek Dioskouroi, Lat. Gemini and Baltic, Germanic and Celtic myths) associated with dawn (Uṣas), rescuers of people in distress, and healers. They are sometimes also called saviours of men and in the Vedic Pantheon they act as the *adhvaryus* of the gods.

***aṣṭākṣara*** 'eight-syllabled'; often used as the name of a widely popular eight-syllabled *mantra* which is addressed to Viṣṇu: *Oṁ nama Nārāyaṇāya*.

***aṣṭaṅga yoga*** the eightfold path of training one's body and mind for the sake of liberation according to Patañjali's system described in the Yoga Sūtras. The eight *aṅgas* are: (1) *yama*, i.e. observance of *ahiṁsā* (non-violence), *satya* (truthfulness), *asteya* (non-stealing), *brahmacarya* (pure living) and *aparigraha* (non-acquisitiveness); (2) *niyama*, i.e. practice of *śauca* (purity), *saṅtoṣa* (contentment), *tapas* (austerity), *svādhyāya* (own study) and *īśvarapraṇidhāna* (lit. 'surrender to God', often interpreted as 'self-surrender'); (3) *āsana* (posture); (4) *prāṇāyāma* (control of the life force, through breath-control); (5) *pratyāhāra* (sense withdrawal); (6) *dharaṇā* (concentration); (7) *dhyāna* (meditation); and (8) *samādhi* (unification).

**Atharva Veda (AV)** the fourth Vedic collection of hymns codified under Brahminic supervision possibly in Magadha around 600 B.C. from older materials, much of them stemming from the tradition of the Vrātyas, who had not previously followed the Vedic tradition. It has some features in common with the early Upaniṣads, e.g. the use of the term *brahman* to denote the highest reality and it was therefore sometimes referred to as Brahma Veda. Because of its Vrātya background, some orthodox brahmins objected to the incorporating of AV into *śruti*, and it took several hundred years before it was universally accepted, but there are still some Brahminic sections who regard it as inferior even today.

**Atharvan** a mythical priest said to have instituted the worship of fire by offering it *soma*.

**ātmajñāna** self-knowledge.

**ātman** self (wrongly: 'soul'). From the Ṛgvedic expression for 'breath' (cf. Gr. *atmos* and Germ. *Atem*) or the 'animating principle' it developed into the most important Upaniṣadic notion of 'inner self', referring to the innermost essence of man which is identical with *brahman*, the essence of reality as a whole and its source. Whoever gains insight into the depths of his nature and becomes fully aware of *ātman* as his innermost core, will also, according to the teaching of the Upaniṣads, realize his identity with *brahman*, the divine source of the whole universe, and thereby reach salvation.

**Auṁ** see Oṁ.

**Aurobindo Ghosh** (1872–1950) Cambridge-educated and destined for the civil service, he became instead a nationalist revolutionary. After a yogic experience during a one-year prison sentence, he settled in French Pondicherry, founded an *āśram* and wrote yogic and philosophical works. He developed his own version of Integral Yoga and in his cosmic philosophy he envisaged the possibility of a new phase in the evolution of the world, provided a certain number of individuals prepared themselves through yoga and a commitment to a spiritual way of life for receiving the cosmic consciousness which could bring about the spiritualization of the whole earth or even universe.

**Auroville** a settlement of followers of Aurobindo, recruited from all over the world, on the east coast of South India, trying to create an alternative life-style to modern civilization with Aurobindo's philosophy as basis.

***avatāra*** descent, advent; descent of god to earth; divine incarnation undertaken for the purpose of assisting the world or mankind in distress or showing it the path to salvation. The first indication of the notion of divine incarnation can be found in the RV when Aditi, the goddess of infinity, who represents the precreational dimension of reality, gave birth to the world, gods and men and then was born into the world as the daughter of one of her sons, the god Dakṣa (10,72,4–5). The teaching was fully spelled out for the first time in the BhG (4,7–8) and elaborated in the Purāṇas, especially in connection with ten main and many minor incarnations of Viṣṇu some of which are, however, in a way foreshadowed in the earlier literature, e.g. in the RV by the three steps of Viṣṇu and in TS and SB by his appearance as a dwarf.

**Avesta** the sacred scripture of Zarathushtra preserved in the Old Iranian language, which is closely akin to the Vedic Sanskrit. It also contains many parallels to Vedic procedures and ideas.

***avidyā*** ignorance: mistaken view about the nature of reality.

***ayam ātmā brahma*** (this self is *brahman*, BU 4,4,5) one of the 'great pronouncements' (*mahāvākyas*) of the Upaniṣads asserting the identity of the inner self with the divine essence of the universe, which is the central theme of the Upaniṣadic teachings. It is further the main tenet of the Advaita Vedānta school of thought and in a modified way also of Viṣiṣta Advaita. It is, moreover, the most widely held view among Hindus, often in a popularized form, namely that God or the Divine dwells in the human heart, in all creatures and in every single thing.

**Ayodhyā** ('invincible'; modern Oudh) the ancient capital of the kingdom from whose royal family came prince Rāma, the hero of the epic Rāmāyaṇa and the seventh incarnation of Viṣṇu. It is one of the seven sacred cities of Hinduism and is located on the banks of the river Gogrā (ancient Śarayū) four miles from Fyzābād, Uttar Pradesh. It has a fortress-like temple of Hanumān and had a temple to Rāma which was converted into a mosque by Bābar, the first Mughal ruler of India.

**Āyur Veda** ('life knowledge') one of the Upavedas and the ancient system of medicine, still practised. It recognizes the atomic theory, the teaching on the three *guṇas*, five elements, seven bodily substances, three sheaths of the body and three humours of temperament.

**Bādarāyaṇa** (some time between 200–450 A.D.) the author of the *Brahma Sūtras*, the basic work of the Vedāntic school of thought notable particularly for the introduction of the *līlā* theory of creation. Composed in the aphoristic *sūtra* style, the work is not easy to understand and several commentaries were written on it, the best known being that of Śaṅkara.

**Balarāma** the elder brother of Kṛṣṇa. He shared in some of his adventures and is regarded as an incarnation of the cosmic snake Śeṣa or a partial incarnation of Viṣṇu. In some parts of India he replaces the Buddha in the icons of the ten major incarnations of Viṣṇu.

**Basava** (twelfth century A.D.) a South Indian religious and social reformer from a brahmin family of Śiva worshippers. At an early age he became disillusioned with traditional orthodox practices and caste discrimination, left home and set about reforming Śaivism, thus becoming the precursor or founder of a new sect which came to be known as the Liṅgāyata or Vīra Śaiva movement. He preached the equality of women, rejected caste rules and distinctions and the hereditary right of brahmins to priesthood as well as their traditional ritual worship. When he reached the position of a minister of state, he persecuted Vaiṣṇavas, Jains and Buddhists, making converts for his new faith. The reaction of orthodoxy to his reforms got him into trouble and he died amidst some confusion.

**Bath** (*snāna*) is an act of bodily and spiritual purification and a ritual obligation for Hindus and is best taken in flowing water (which perhaps explains the Indian custom of pouring water over oneself when washing in the domestic setting). It is often accompanied by oblation and other rituals and finished with total immersion (*majjana*) if possible. Bathing in sacred rivers, and particularly in Gaṅgā, has further religious significance: in the belief of many, it washes away all guilt.

**Bāuls** wandering religious poets-singers who form a loose sect within the *bhakti* movement. Their beginnings are usually derived from Caitanya's activities, but there are reasons to regard them as being of a more ancient origin. There are recognizable traces of Buddhist Tantric attitudes and practices in their unstructured *sādhanā*. Some of them roam in groups of three, one being a female dancer, and are reminiscent of the ancient Vrātya teams. Some Bāul songs and poems were already collected in the last century and inspired the poetry of Rabindranath Tagore.

**Benares** see Vārāṇasī.

**Besant, Annie Wood** (1847–1933) originally a free thinker, pacifist and socialist, she joined the Theosophical Society in England in 1889 after she reviewed H. P. Blavatsky's monumental work, *The Secret Doctrine*, and in 1893 she moved to India and became the president of the Society in 1907. She founded the Central Hindu School in Vārāṇasī which later became a College and received University status in 1915. She also promoted Indian classical dance. She sought to raise the self-confidence of the Hindu mind in face of Christian missionary activities and was active also in the political field. In 1917 she was even elected to chair the Indian National Congress which earned her temporary internment by the British administration. She wrote several books on Theosophical teachings which overlap in many areas with those of Hinduism.

**Bhaga** one of the Ādityas, representing the quality of bestowing or giving, charity and goodness ('godness': cf. Slav. *bhogu*, *bog*, meaning 'God').

**Bhagavad Gītā** (BhG, the 'Song of the Lord') one of the best known religious works of the world, it is an insertion into the epic of Mhb in the form of a conversation between Arjuna and Kṛṣṇa which took place on the battlefield of Kurukṣetra before the start of the great war. It popularizes the Upaniṣadic teachings and yoga and its main message concerns the method of disinterested action in fulfilling one's duties, while still pursuing the path to salvation. It adopts a strong theistic stance and spells out for the first time the teaching on periodic divine incarnations on earth to help restore truth or righteousness in times of its decline. Its date is uncertain, but it can hardly be earlier than 200 B.C. or later than A.D. 400.

**Bhagavān** (derived from the name of the Āditya Bhaga) the Lord; Reverend; Venerable. This title is usually reserved for Kṛṣṇa in historical Hinduism, but later it began to be used for other deities and for the Buddha and was even usurped by self-styled *gurus* (e.g. Rajneesh).

**Bhāgavata** a devotee of the Bhagavān i.e. of the Lord Kṛṣṇa. The cult started developing into a sectarian movement of Bhāgavatas within Vaiṣṇavism from about 100 B.C.

**Bhairava** a wrathful incarnation of Śiva; Bhairavī: his consort.

***bhajan(a)*** (sharing, service, worship; it is derived from the Skt. root *bhaj*, just as *bhakti*) - devotional song.

***bhakta*** a devotee pursuing the path of love for God.

***bhakti*** love, devotion. Often depicted in some Purāṇas as an overpowering emotion, it can be adopted as an exclusive goal of life, a way to God (*bhaktimārga*). It is also often regarded as a way of life which can be rationally and deliberately cultivated and it then becomes a 'discipline of devotion' (Bhakti Yoga).

***bhang*** (vern., Skt. *bhaṅgā*) a narcotic from a herb, *Cannabis sativa*, whose leaves are used for smoking and taken to induce altered states of consciousness by some sectarian *sādhus*.

**Bharata** the name of several ancient Āryan personalities and of a powerful tribe which took part in the great war described in the epos Mbh and gave it its name. It has also been adopted as the name for the Republic of India (Bharat).

**Bharata Nāṭya** a classical dance form which originated in South Indian temples where it was performed by *devadāsis*. Many of its poses are represented by sculptures on the temple in Chidambaram and some on the Sun temple in Konārak which helped in the modern reconstruction of the nearly forgotten dance form.

**Bhāratavarṣa** the ancient name of (North) India.

**Bharatiya Vidya Bhavan** a cultural and educational organization founded by Dr. K. M. Munshi in 1938, with headquarters in Bombay and branches in some two dozen Indian cities and one in London. Its proclaimed aims are the spiritual regeneration of India and its Sanskrit culture. Although not overtly religious, its underlying philosophy is nourished by Hindu ideals with strong universalistic tendencies.

***bhava*** existence, being, becoming.

**Bhava** a deity representing positive values of existence; the lord of cattle and men, a benign form of Śiva as giver of existence.

**Bhavānī** one of the names of Śiva's consort; the name often used for the Devī in Śākta cults.

***bheda*** difference, distinction, cleavage; a term used by some schools of Vedāntic philosophy when discussing the problem of the difference between the world and *brahman* or between the individual and God.

**Bhedābheda** ('distinction – non-distinction'; fr. *bheda-abheda*) a Vedāntic doctrine formulated by Nimbārka, and known also as Dvaitādvaita, according to which the world and individual beings are both different and non-different from God or *brahman*. The school later flourished in Kashmir.

***bhikṣu*** mendicant; another name applied sometimes to the fourth stage of life *(saṁnyāsa); Buddhist monk.*

***bhūmi*** earth; level of existence; stage of spiritual achievement; in Buddhism: a stage on the *bodhisattva* path.

***bhūr(r)loka*** the terrestrial world and the underworld.

***bhūta*** a category of malicious spirits, subordinate to Śiva.

***bhuvana*** the world, universe; level of existence.

**Bhuvaneśa** the name of Ganeśa in his aspect as the Lord of the world, depicted with eight arms.

**Bhuvaneśvara** (the 'lord of the world') a title of Śiva; the capital city of Orissa (Bhubaneshwar) renowned for its large number of Hindu temples dating from A.D. 750–1100 which escaped destruction by Muslim invaders and are therefore of great importance for the study of the development of Hindu temple architecture.

**Bhuvaneśvarī** the title of the Devī in Śākta cults.

***bhuvarloka*** intermediary world (Vedic *antarikṣa*) between earth and heaven (or material and spiritual worlds).

***bīja*** seed; *bīja mantra*: 'seminal *mantra*', which is always monosyllabic and is used mostly in Tantric systems.

***bilva*** (vern. ***bel***) a tree, *Aegle marmelos*, from whose wood Śiva made his staff (*bilvadaṇḍa*) and therefore it is favoured as material for making amulets. It also provides ingredients for medicines and oaths are sworn by it.

***bindu*** dot, drop, globule; in philosophy: the metaphysical point out of time and space where the absolute and the phenomenal meet, which is experienced in some types of *samādhi*; the sacred mark made on the forehead, symbolizing the third eye (the eye of wisdom); in the Tantras: semen; Śiva's semen, the essence of life and the symbol of the nectar of immortality; the symbol of *brahman*, the essence of all reality.

**Birth in Hinduism** is never the beginning of life of a new being, but the rebirth of one who is transmigrating from life to life.

**Blavatsky, Helena Petrovna** (1831–91) the cofounder, with Colonel Olcott, of the Theosophical Society, in 1875, and the author of voluminous works based on Hindu and Buddhist teachings which had some influence on the neo-Hindu reform movements.

***bodhisattva***, Bodhisattva ('enlightenment being') a being destined for enlightenment; a being whose essence is enlightenment. It is a Buddhist term designating, in the first place, a person who took a vow not to rest content with personal liberation, but to train for the full enlightenment of a Buddha in order to show also other beings the path to freedom. In Mahāyāna Buddhism it also means a person who, on the threshold of *nirvāṇa*, renounces personal liberation to stay in the world as long as there are beings suffering in *saṁsāra* who need assistance. When the doctrine of transcendental Buddhas emerged, 'celestial' Bodhisattvas appeared in their retinue as their projections, acting as their mediators in the world. Some of them have names shared with Hindu deities and have come to be worshipped by both Buddhists and Hindus, each of the two flocks having a somewhat different perception of them and their nature.

**Body** a complex structure composed of progressively finer layers, defined somewhat differently from school to school.

Generally speaking, there is (1) the gross body (*sthūla śarīra*) of physiological functions; (2) the subtle body (*sūkṣma śarīra*), itself formed by several 'sheaths' (*kośas*), which has its own subtle physiology and is the conductor of the life force (*prāṇa*) and the scene of mental processes; and (3) the 'causal' body (*liṅga śarīra*, sometimes also called *kāraṇa śarīra*) which stores the imprints of *karma* and the pattern of the personal character qualities (*vāsanas*) and transmigrates from life to life. The Vedāntic system recognizes five layers or sheaths (*kośas*) of personality: *annamaya*, *prāṇamaya*, *manomaya*, *vijñānamaya* and *ānandamaya*.

**Brahma, Brahmā** the chief god during the period of Brāhmanism. He was then virtually co-existent with the Upaniṣadic divine source of reality, the *brahman*, as Self-existent God and called Brahman Svayaṁbhū (BU 2,6,3). He lost much of his importance and following when he became merely the God 'Creator', the first of the Hindu Trinity (Trimūrti), with Viṣṇu as the Preserver and active ruler of the universe and Śiva as the Destroyer (but also the Lord of Yoga). Reduced to playing an active part only at the beginning of the world cycle, he is often thought of as sunk in cosmic slumber or deep meditation and has to be awakened if he is needed. He is depicted with four heads, bearded, and with four arms. His wife is Sarasvati, originally his daughter, and his mount is the goose or swan (*haṁsa*). He has only two temples dedicated to him in India (in Puṣkara near Ajmere and in Khedbrahmā), and he has a bathing *ghāṭ* at Bithūr.

***brahmacarya*** ('divine faring') following a discipline for the sake of the realization of the ultimate goal. While in some systems its meaning is narrowed down to 'celibacy', as e.g. in the *yamas* in Patañjali's *aṣṭaṅga yoga*, in Tantric systems it may even involve ritual *maithuna*; also: discipleship or apprenticeship as the first *āśrama* or stage of life in the ancient Aryan scheme, usually lasting twelve years and spent in the house of the teacher; hence *brahmacāri*: pupil, disciple, apprentice; one following the life of a spiritual discipline.

***brahman*, Brahman** the transcendental divine source and at the same time the innermost essence of all reality, identical to *ātman*, first fully defined in this way in the Uppaniṣads. In the early

Vedic period *brahman* designated the mysterious power of *mantras*, sacrificial formulae and prayer, but gradually its meaning deepened, no doubt under the influence of the AV where it denoted the highest reality. In Śaṅkara's Advaita Vedānta *brahman* is asserted as the sole reality, while the multiplicity of the experienced manifested reality, including individual selves, is regarded as a product of illusion (*māyā*), born out of ignorance (*avidyā*).

***brāhmaṇa, brahman, brāhman, brahmin*** priest; a member of the first of the four hereditary castes.

**Brāhmaṇas** priestly books, treatises on liturgy and its mythological and cosmic significance. The most important one is Śatapatha Brāhmaṇa (SB).

**Brahmanaspati, Bṛhaspati** 'the Lord of *brahman*' in the sense of prayer and magic or ritual formula; he is a Vedic god, regarded as the chief priest of the gods, and the precursor of Brahma.

**Brāhmanism** (adj. Brāhmanic, Brahminic) the period in the development of Indian religions which was marked by the dominating influence of brahmins and their ritualistic outlook. It was preceded by 'Vedism' and followed by the Upaniṣadic revival of spiritual endeavours.

***brahmarṣi*** a seer or sage of Brahminic origin.

**Brahma Sūtras of Bādarāyaṇa** the earliest source of the Vedāntic school of philosophy possibly composed between A.D. 200–450.

**Brahma Veda** another name for the AV.

**Brahma Vidyā** knowledge of the ultimate reality; theology.

***brahma vihāra*** ('divine abode') the designation for a meditative achievement, a state of mind, known to the Buddhist system and to Patañjali's Yoga system. It has four stages.

***brāhmī*** an early form of writing derived from a Semitic source which was used in Aśoka's rock edicts and developed later into *devanāgarī* script.

**Brāhmo Samaj** a reform movement founded on 20.8.1828 by R. M. Roy (first as Brahma Sabhā), a kind of Hindu equivalent of European Unitarianism. It stressed the unity of God, rejected priesthood, sacrifices, representations of God, the caste system and the teaching of reincarnation. It was supported by three generations of the Tagore family, then influenced for a time by K. S. Sen and it survives as a relatively small but progressive sect mainly in West Bengal.

**Bṛhadāraṇyaka Upaniṣad** one of the most important Upaniṣads, belonging to the White YV, pre-Buddhist, ascribed to Yājñavalkya.

**Bṛhad-Devatā** a summary of the deities and myths of the RV ascribed to Śaunaka, probably composed in the fifth century B.C.

**Buddha** (the Enlightened or the Awakened One; cca 563–483 B.C.) a title or a designation for a man, in early Buddhist sources described as prince Siddhattha Gotama of the Sakya clan, who reached enlightenment and became the teacher of 'gods and men', showing them the way out from the chain of lives in *saṁsāra* to the final state of liberation called *nirvāṇa* (Pl. *nibbāna*). Although he may not have intended to part entirely with the Vedic-Brahminic tradition, at least as far as its spiritual message is concerned, an independent religious and monastic movement developed in his wake and dominated much of India for several centuries, virtually finishing off the period of Brāhmanism. After the decline of Buddhism and the revival of the previous Brahminic tradition in the new garb of Hinduism, much of what the Buddha had taught was incorporated into the broadened Hindu outlook and the Buddha was even included in the Hindu Pantheon in some Purāṇas as the ninth incarnation of Viṣṇu, although some resistance to him has remained in evidence in some quarters, backed by conservative brahmins, mainly because of his disregard for the hereditary caste system and his denial of the divine origin of the Vedas. Mahāyāna Buddhism later developed a sophisticated doctrine of transcendental and Cosmic Buddhas, emanations of Ādi Buddha, accompanied by a retinue of Bodhisattvas, their own emanations. There are overlaps of this doctrine with some sectarian teachings in Hinduism, particularly in the Tantric context.

***buddhi*, Buddhi** higher mind; intelligence; higher cognition; the first cosmic evolute of *prakṛti* in the Sāṅkhya philosophy.

**Buddhism** the religious tradition derived from the teachings of the Buddha which has grown into a world religion with several schools of philosophy, some major and minor sects and a variety of religious observances and spiritual practices.

***budha*** 'wise, intelligent'.

**Budha** the planet Mercury; also the name of a Vedic *ṛṣi*.

***caitanya*** consciousness, intelligence; supreme consciousness.

**Caitanya** (1486–1533) a Bengali ecstatic and representative of *bhakti* Vaiṣṇavism, combined with Sahajiyā elements, and a great devotee of Kṛṣṇa. His full initiation name is Śrīkṛṣṇacaitanya. After his years as a wanderer he lived mostly in Puri where he used to lead the singers and dancers accompanying the Jagannātha processions. A sectarian tradition grew in his wake, with a theology steeped in Madhva's tradition, but popularized in poetry and through Caitanya's legendary biography, which promoted him to a full incarnation of Kṛṣṇa.

***caitya*** individual consciousness or 'soul'; a shrine or place of worship; a pile of stones as a landmark; monument; a burial mound; a Buddhist stūpa.

***cakra*** wheel; discus; centre of spiritual faculties in the subtle body distributed along the central duct parallel to the spine, as taught in the system of Kuṇḍalinī Yoga: there are six of them in number: *mūlādhāra (root-holding) cakra* at the base of the spine; *svādhiṣṭhāna* (self-based) *cakra* opposite the generative organs; *maṇipūra* (gem-filled) *cakra* opposite the navel; *anāhata* (unstuck or 'silent sound') *cakra* opposite the central point of the chest; *viśuddha* (purified) *cakra* opposite the throat; and *ājñā* (command) *cakra* between the eyebrows. The seventh and highest spiritual centre is called *sahasrāra padma* (thousand-petalled lotus) and is on top of or just above the skull. For symbolical meanings see Wheel.

***cakravartin*** ('wheel-turner') world-governing righteous monarch; Emperor; spiritual world-teacher; a Buddha. Cf. Wheel.

**Calendar** had never quite been unified throughout India before the adoption of the European system. The basis of the Hindu year is a lunar month (which begins with the full moon in the North and with the new moon in the South), divided into the bright half (*śulapakṣa*), starting with the new moon, and the dark half (*kṛṣṇapakṣa*), starting with the full moon. There are twelve lunar months divided into six seasons (*ṛtu*):

Vasanta (spring): Caitra (March/April), Vaiśakha (April/May);
Grīṣma (hot season): Jyaiṣṭha (May/June), Aṣāḍha (June/July);
Varṣa (rainy season): Śrāvaṇa (July/August), Bhādrapada (August/September);
Śarad (autumn): Aśvinā, Āśvayuja (September/October), Kārttika (October/November);
Hemanta (winter): Mārgaśīrṣa (November/December), Pauṣa (December/January);
Śiśira (frosty season): Māgha (January/February), Phālguna (February/March).

A thirteenth month is added every two or three years to make up for the difference between the lunar and the solar year. In some parts of India the year starts with Kārttika or even some other month. The Western solar calendar had been known since Gupta times and was sometimes used alongside the lunar one for accuracy. Since colonial times the Hindu calendar has been used only for religious purposes and in astrology.

**Cālukya** (Chalukya) a dynasty in the Deccan (cca 550–753 A.D.) whose capital was Badāmi and whose fame reached as far as Persia. They were great builders and erected some of the earliest known Hindu temples at Aihole and in Badāmi. In

Badāmi they also dedicated rock-carved shrines to Śiva and Viṣṇu. One of them contains a highly artistic image of Viṣṇu sitting on the coils of the cosmic serpent Ananta. They had originally expanded by defeating the Pallavas and in the end were themselves overthrown by the Rāṣṭrakūtas.

**Cāmuṇḍā, Cāmuṇḍī** a terrifying emanation of Durgā from her forehead for the purpose of killing the demons Chaṇḍa and Muṇḍa.

***caṇḍāla*** an outcast; an untouchable; sometimes used in the narrow sense for the 'subcaste' of the untouchables engaged in washing and clothing corpses and carrying them to the burning *ghāṭs*.

**Candella** (Chandella) a Rājput dynasty which flourished from 800–1204. Its rulers were builders and patrons of the Khajurāho temple complex.

**Candī, Candika** one of the names of the goddess Kālī.

**Caṇḍīdās** (fourteenth century) a Bengali *bhakta* and poet with Sahajiyā background who greatly influenced Caitanya.

***candra*** moon; Candra: the Moon god.

**Cārvāka** the legendary teacher of materialist philosophy; in pl.: followers of that philosophy.

**Caste** at the root of the Indian caste system is the IE division of society into three classes of (1) warriors and aristocrats, (2) priesthood and (3) professional and working people. When the Indo-Āryans colonized Northern India, a fourth, subservient class of conquered original inhabitants was added, and since they were of darker colour, a stronger, because racial, barrier divided them from the three higher classes. This had its repercussions in strengthening the divisions between the three higher classes and it became one of the causes for the classes to turn into four rigid castes (Skt. *varṇa*, meaning 'colour'): *brāhmaṇa* (brahmin, priest), *kṣatriya* (ruler, aristocrat, warrior), *vaiśya* (merchant, craftsman, peasant etc.) and *śūdra* (labourer, servant), besides outcasts doing unclean tasks, recruited from the lowest classes of the subdued Non-Āryans, some prisoners of war and some primitive tribal communities. Brahmins usurped first rank on account of their function as mediators between men and gods, but real power rested with the rulers. Brahmins also sanctioned castes as divinely ordained in the process of the creation of the world (cf. RV 10,90). Further divisions came about over the centuries as a result of mixed marriages, and offspring from intercourse with lower caste concubines and casual intercourse across the caste barriers, and also as a result of occupations becoming hereditary and forming sub-castes (*jāti*). At one time the caste system seemed inseparable from Hinduism as did feudalism from Christianity, but modern neo-Hindu reformers condemned the system and after independence in 1947 the caste system was abolished by law, although it still largely survives as a strong tradition and social prejudice not only in India, but even in many emigrant Hindu communities throughout the world. It is no longer possible, however, to regard it as an essential or necessary feature of Hinduism.

***celā*** (vern.) pupil, disciple of a *guru*.

**Chāndogya Upaniṣad** one of the most important early Upaniṣads, pre-Buddhist, belonging to SV.

**Chatterjee, Bankim Chandra** (1838–94) a novelist who promoted religious and nationalist feelings and influenced the early part of Aurobindo's life. He was the author of the poem 'Bande Mātaram', originally meant as a hymn to Kālī, which became the Indian national anthem.

**Churning the ocean** a Purāṇic mythological story which was already known in some form in Vedic times (cf. RV 10,136). Gods and demons (*asuras*) joined forces to churn the waters of the cosmic ocean (symbolizing space, the ether or the primeval element of the 'void' which is the womb of everything that ever emerges in the world in the course of its manifestation and duration) in order to obtain the drink of immortality (*amṛta*) from it. Various other gifts and products were churned out first, both beneficial, e.g. the goddess Śrī or Lakṣmī, and detrimental, e.g. the deadly poison Halāhala which threatened to destroy all life. All living beings were saved by Śiva who, as Yogapati, was already immortal and drank the poison, suffering merely a discolouration of his throat. The reference to this feat in the above-mentioned hymn of the RV is the first indication of the notion of a Saviour God (named Rudra in the hymn); and he is joined, in the Vedic record, in drinking from the cup of poison by the long-haired accomplished sage (see *keśin*), the gentle helper of beings and the prototype of originally human, but perfected saints who voluntarily undergo suffering to bring salvation to others. On the higher (i.e. *ādhyātmika*) level of interpretation, the world ocean represents the mind, its churning symbolizes the process of meditation, the preliminary gifts and products represent higher blissful states of consciousness and by-products of yoga such as magic powers, which can be as dangerous as poison, and the resulting product, the nectar of immortality, represents liberation.

***cintāmaṇi*** ('wish-gem') a jewel granting all wishes. It is in the possession of Brahma.

***cit*** consciousness; the middle part of the compound *saccidānanda*, the Advaitic designation for the experience of the absolute reality.

***citta*** heart, mind; 'heart and soul'; mentality, character.

**Coḻa** (Chola) a South Indian dynasty (ninth to fourteenth century) who succeeded the Pallavas (weakened by wars with Cālukyas) and at one time dominated Sri Lanka. They built several famous temples in South Indian style, among them one in Tanjore dedicated to Śiva.

**Cosmic ocean** see Āpas and Churning the ocean.

**Cosmogony** (the story of the origin of the universe) is expressed in several Vedic and Purāṇic creation myths, in popular legends and also in philosophical texts foreshadowed in the 'Creation hymn' (RV 10,129). It is envisaged not as a creation out of nothing, but as a continuous process of periodic manifestations (*sṛṣṭi*) of the universe out of its divine source or the dimension of the unmanifest, and it has its duration for a time (*sthiti*) which is followed by the dissolution (*laya*) of the manifested world back into the hidden source, only to re-emerge again and again in ever-recurring cycles. This process has no conceivable beginning in time. However, since time is philosophically conceived not as an absolute measure which would express itself in a linear movement from an infinite past to an infinite future, but as a relative element which is itself a part of the cycle of manifestation, the divine transcendent source is beyond it and remains unaffected by the cycles of the manifestation of the universe. This picture would be compatible with the modern astrophysical theories of a 'pulsating universe' periodically expanding after a 'big bang' and then again collapsing.

**Cosmology** (the description of the universe and its history) has evolved in Indian mythology in several versions which share a certain general structure. Thus our own universe is described as egg-shaped and as being only one among many (which reminds one of Einstein's circular universe and of the large number of galaxies known to astronomy). In Hindu understanding the world not only has physical reality, but comprises several dimensions which range from gross-material ones to purely spiritual ones. The earth plane is central in this hierarchy of existential dimensions, with its humans, animals and also invisible spirits. Above are six divisions of heaven (*svarga*), below seven divisions of the nether world (*pātala*) with mythical inhabitants, and in the bottom part there are seven zones of the temporary hell or purgatory (*naraka*). Between world systems there is empty space (which, however, may also be inhabited by beings temporarily trapped there by their karmic destiny). The duration of one universe on the relative time scale equals, according to Purāṇic reckoning, the life-span of its ruler, Brahma; he lives 100 Brahmic years, which represent 311,040,000 million human years. One day of Brahma is a *kalpa* and represents one cycle in the life of the universe equal to 4,320 million years, followed by a period of rest during Brahma's night when the world and beings are in a state of suspension. Brahma's death is followed by a great cosmic night (*mahārātri*) when worlds and beings are reabsorbed into the divine source to be sent forth again at the beginning of the new manifestation which starts with the birth of a new Brahma. One day of Brahma, i.e. one world period or *kalpa*, is divided into 1000 *mahāyugas*; each of these lasts 4,320,000 years and is further divided into four *yugas* or ages of world history with progressively worsening conditions of life: Kṛta (1,728,000 years), Tretā (1,296,000 years), Dvāpara (864,000 years) and Kali Yuga (432,000), the present age.

**Cow** from a prized domestic animal yielding nourishing and useful products she developed into a sacred object of veneration and a symbol of Mother Earth and even of the cosmic Great Mother Aditi, although in pre-Āryan times it was the bull that was associated with sacred symbolism as can still be seen in the Mauryan emblem (cf. the capitals of Aśoka's columns) and in Śiva's mount and emblem, the Nandi. The cow was regarded as sacred from around the time of the Guptas and killing one became a capital offence. She has preserved much of her privileged and protected status up to the present day, being allowed to roam freely even in cities among all the traffic.

**Creation**, in the sense of an initial creative act of God giving rise to the world out of nothing, does not apply in Hinduism. Whenever the word is used, it refers to the beginning of one of the many periodic manifestations of the world; see Cosmogony.

**Cremation** is virtually the only accepted way in Hinduism of disposing of the bodies of deceased persons, described or at least mentioned in even the earliest parts of the Vedas. It is undoubtedly of IE origin. Early archaeological evidence of burials may be ascribed to indigenous, pre-Āryan, strata.

**Daityas** sons of the Vedic goddess Diti who later became adversaries of *devas*, hence regarded as demons.

***dākiṇī*** a class of female goblins in the retinue of Kālī; in Tantric sects: a female partner in left-hand rituals; and also in Tantric left-hand yoga practice.

**Dākiṇī** a Tantric goddess of mystic wisdom.

**Dakṣa** one of the Ādityas, the god of skill, dexterity and intelligence. While being the son of Aditi, the primordial mother of all beings and the source of the world, he is also said to have become the father of Aditi when she was born into the world, perhaps the first intimation of the doctrine of divine incarnations which developed later. His other daughter was Diti, the goddess of manifested space. In the epic and Purāṇic time Dakṣa was regarded as the son of Brahma and an incarnation of Viṣṇu.

***dakṣiṇa*** southern, right, right-handed; auspicious; male.

***dakṣiṇā*** the portion of the sacrifice which goes to the officiating brahmin as his share.

***dakṣiṇācāri*** the follower of the right-hand Tantric practice.

**Dakṣinā Mūrti** Śiva's effigy as the Great Yogi.

**Dakṣināpati** 'lord of the South', a title of Yama.

***ḍamaru*** drum: a small double-sided drum shaped like an hour-glass which is carried by Śiva as Naṭarāja. It symbolizes the primeval sound of the manifesting universe and its rhythmic pulsing, which is based on polarity: the upper half of the drum represents the *liṅga* and the lower one the *yoni*.

***dāna*** gift, donation; almsgiving.

**Dance** (*nātya*, vern. *nāc*) is believed to have originated with Śiva and his *tāṇḍava*, the cosmic dance of destruction and renewal. His wife Pārvatī complemented it with a seductive feminine dance (*lāsya*). This indicates the religious origin of dance which in reality probably developed from ceremonial steps and movements of priests and their attendants during the sacrificial ritual and was subsequently transformed into temple dancing performed by *devadāsis* to please gods and pilgrims. This practice was current in some temples, especially in South India, until well into the nineteenth century, although it suffered limitations under Islamic rulers when court and secular dancing was more favoured and the dancing profession acquired a dubious reputation (cf. the associations with the term 'nautch' girls). The modern secular revival of classical and folk dancing has placed it on the level of a performing art of high standard. The religious dancing of the *bhaktas* celebrating the divine *līlā* can still be seen on occasion.

***daṇḍa*** staff, rod, sceptre; punishment; discipline; cosmic law; universal order; the king's right and duty to enforce law and order by punishments as the chief principle of state management (the failure to use it was believed to lead to the decline of civilization).

**Daṇḍadhara** Yama's title as the judge of the dead.

***darśana*** 'seeing', viewing, point of view; seeing the ultimate truth, either by one's own experience or 'by proxy' when going to see an accomplished *guru* or saint or a famous effigy of a god ('having a darshan' may nowadays also refer to going to see any person reputed or claiming to have higher spiritual knowledge); the designation given to each of the six main or 'classical' schools of Hindu 'orthodox' philosophy: Sāṅkhya, Yoga, Nyāya, Vaiśeṣika, Pūrva-Mīmāṁsā and Uttara-Mīmāṁsā (Vedānta).

**Dāsa, Dasyu** terms used in the RV for the pre-Āryan population opposing the Āryan invasions, described as dark-skinned.

***dāsa***, (f. *dāsī*) slave (in post-Vedic Sanskrit texts).

**Daśahrā** (vern. Dussehra) the ten day festival, celebrated from the first till the tenth day of the bright half of the month Āśvina (September/October) in honour of Durgā and her victory over the demon-king Mahiṣāsura and/or of Rāma and his victory over Rāvaṇa, the demon-king of Laṅkā, and the recovery of his wife Sītā from captivity. The latter is celebrated with dramatic performances of Rāmlīlā based on the story of Rāma's life by Tulsīdās.

**Daśanāmī Order** ('having ten names') a federation of communities of *saṅnyāsis* tracing their origin to Śaṅkara. It has four main monastic colleges, centres of Advaitic learning and practice, in four quarters of India: W – at Dvārakā, E – in Purī, N – in Badri and S – in Śṛṅgeri. It is supposed to have ten branches whose names are: (1) Sārasvatī ('pool'), (2) Purī ('citadel'), (3) Vana ('tree'), (4) Tīrtha ('ford'), (5) Giri ('hill') (6) Parvata ('mountain'), (7) Bhāratī ('country'), (8) Araṇya ('forest'), (9) Āśrama ('hermitage'), and (10) Sagara ('sea'). There is little research on the distribution and actual organization of these branches.

**Daśāvatāra** the icon of the ten main incarnations of Viṣṇu, representing Matsya (fish), Kūrma (turtle), Varāha (boar), Narasimha (man-lion), Vāmana (dwarf), Paraśurāma (Rāma the hero with the axe), Rama (Rama the prince), Kṛṣṇa (Kṛṣṇa the pastoral god, later the revealer of the BhG), Buddha (Buddha the world teacher and destroyer of demons, often replaced by Balarāma, the elder brother of Krsna) and Kalki (the future saviour).

**Dayānanda** (1824–83) the founder of Ārya Samāj He advocated the purging from Hinduism of 'Purānic and epic ballast' and the return to the pure tradition of the four Vedas which he held as infallible and containing all knowledge, including modern Western ideas and even inventions. He also advocated the basically sound principle of interpreting the Vedas on at least three levels (*ādhyātmika*, *ādhidaivika* and *ādhibhautika*) as expounded in Yāska's *Nirukta*. His teaching was a kind of underlying monism manifested in three principles, namely God, *puruṣa* and *prakṛti*. He opposed animal sacrifices and although he did not oppose the caste system, he worked for the upgrading of the status of the lower castes and the outcasts. Although not admitting it, he was influenced to a considerable degree by European liberal ideas.

**Death** in Hindu belief is not the end of life for the individual, but is followed by a new life shaped by previous actions and by the degree of mental development or decline in the course of continuous transmigration.

***deha*** body; *dehi* ('one who has a body'): one of the designations for the individual *ātman* or individual 'soul' (*jīvātman*).

***deva***, (cf. Lat. *deus*) god; a category of beings inhabiting the celestial planes of existence (*devaloka*), with a hierarchical structure which is not rigidly determined, so that the status and function of individual gods may undergo many variations; the expression is also often used for nature spirits, living in trees and other natural habitats.

***devadāsī*** ('slave of god') female temple dancer. The training in temple dancing and erotic arts, which often went with it, started at the age of seven or eight. The dancer was then married to the god of the temple or to the *pīpal* tree in the temple precinct. The marriage itself was consummated by the priest or on a stone *liṅga*. Temple dancers often also bestowed sexual favours on pilgrims for the benefit of the temple finances. The tradition of temple dancers was discontinued towards the end of the last century.

**Devakī** the mother of Kṛṣṇa, regarded sometimes as an incarnation of Aditi.

***devaloka*** the world of gods ruled by Indra; heaven.

***devanāgarī*** (the script 'of the city of the gods') the Sanskrit script developed from an earlier form called *brāhmī*. It is used also for Hindī and some other modern Indian languages.

***devarṣi*** an accomplished seer or sage who can dwell in celestial abodes in the company of gods.

***devatā*** deity; applied mainly to lower household and sylvan gods and spirits of the elements.

***devayāna*** the mystical 'way of the gods' travelled after death by humans who strive for the highest spiritual goal. They are supposed to reach immortality via the solar sphere and the Brahmaloka. The passage through its several stages, described in some Upaniṣads, represents a symbolical progress to salvation.

***devī*** goddess; Devī: the great Goddess of the Śākta tradition, i.e. of the cult of the feminine principle which is embodied in many female deities when they are conceived as dominant figures, the most prominent being the figures of Durgā and Kālī.

She is also identified with *prakṛti* (nature) and as such appears in folk representations both in the form of the benign and caring mother of creation and in her aspect of a terrifying and bloodthirsty goddess bringing catastrophes.

**Dhanur Veda** the art of archery (an Upaveda).

***dhāraṇā*** (holding) concentration; fixing attention on one object; the sixth limb of Patañjali's eightfold yoga.

***dhāraṇī*** a composite *mantra*; a charm; a protective spell in the form of a spoken formula.

**Dharaṇī** the earth; the Earth goddess.

***dharma*** righteousness, virtue, integrity; discipline; duty, caste duty; reality, truth, cosmic law; *āśrama dharma*: primary pursuit and duty appropriate to the stage of life (*āśrama*) one is in (a somewhat artificial Brahminic attempt to combine the scheme of four *āśramas* with that of four *puruṣārthas*): (1) the discipline of learning (*brahmacarya*) from and serving one's teacher as a disciple (*brahmacāri*); (2) sensory and aesthetic fulfilment (*kāma*) and the satisfaction of material and social ambitions (*artha*) as a householder (*gṛhastha*); (3) the discipline of renunciation (*saṁnyāsa*) and aspiration to achieve liberation (*mokṣa*) as a forest-dwelling hermit (*vānaprastha*); and (4) the final push for liberation (*mokṣa*) as a homeless wanderer (*parivrājaka*, *bhikṣu*, *saṁnyāsi*). Another artificial creation is the term *svadharma* ('own duty') coined relatively late and meaning: duty according to one's caste, stage of life, or (in a rather modern liberal interpretation) even according to one's own understanding of one's position and of the best future course to be adopted on the way to the final goal.

***dharmarāja*** ('king of righteousness, righteous king') an honorific title; the title of Yama, the king and judge of the dead.

**Dharma Śāstra** law book. There are several ancient law books which go under various names such as Manu and Yājñavalkya.

**Dhātar** one of the Ādityas, the Vedic 'establisher' or 'holder' of the world who assisted in fashioning the universe and its laws. He is the protector of life and family.

***dhoti*** a piece of cloth wrapped round the loins, a traditional form of male clothing worn by Hindus. Some Hindu temples allow entry to men only if they wear a *dhoti* and nothing else, i.e. go barefooted and naked down to their waist.

***dhvaja*** banner, flag, votive column with the mount of the deity to whom the column belongs; symbol of the world axis.

***dhyāna*** meditation, contemplation; mental absorption; the seventh limb of *aṣṭaṅga yoga* of Patañjali.

***digaṁbara*** ('clad in space') a naked mendicant; a Jain monk of the naked sect.

**Digambara** a title of Śiva, who frequently went about naked when practising asceticism.

**Dikpāla** see Lokapāla.

***dīkṣā*** initiation. In the early times of Brāhmanism the term referred to a special set of rituals which included a symbolic sacrifice of the sacrificer's mortal body and aimed at creating for him an immortal body in a kind of second birth. It was possibly a Brahminic ritual emulation of the spiritual rebirth of the ancient *ṛṣis* on their path to immortality. Few could afford this elaborate ritual involving a year of preparation. Most Āryans had to be satisfied with a 'second birth' into their caste (see *upanayana*). In the later times of renewal and the incorporation of the ancient and unorthodox spiritual traditions into Hinduism, the term refers to the initiation of the pupil into higher spiritual practices by his *guru*. In Tantric movements it is again accompanied by symbolic rituals.

**Dīpavālī, Dīvālī** the festival of light which is celebrated all over India in the lunar month of Kārttika (October/November) and is a merger of many different traditions. It is usually associated with

Lakṣmī and the beginning of the new year, after the rainy season, when the sun is welcomed again.

**Diti** the Vedic goddess of manifested space, a complement to Aditi, the goddess of the unmanifest. In the epic and Purāṇic time she is the daughter of Dakṣa and mother of Daityas.

***draṣṭṛ, drastar*** the on-looker or looker on, an expression, used mainly in Vedāntic literature, for the true self as the silent witness of the actions of the external personality of man.

**Drāviḍa, Dravidian** the name for the non-Āryan population (and languages) of India, of ancient Mediterranean origin, who once formed the bulk of the Harappan population before the Āryan invasion. They are now prevalent only in South India, although there is a pocket of people speaking Brahui, a Dravidian language, in Baluchistān. There are four main Dravidian nationalities and languages in South India: Tamil, Kannada (Kanarese), Telagu and Malayalam.

**Dreaming**, or sleep with dreams (*svapna* or *supti*), in which one perceives another world and moves in space with objects and other beings in it, is used in the Upaniṣads and Vedāntic texts as an illustration of the capacity of the mind to project its own images as a seemingly independent external reality outside oneself, by implication rendering the world in the waking state (*jāgarita sthāna*) equally dependent on the mind. Some texts even regard the dreaming state as superior to the waking one and point to methods of mastering the dream process and thereby entering into another dimension of reality with the ability to act consciously and purposefully in it.

***dṛg, dṛk*** the one who sees, a Vedāntic expression for the true self of man.

***dṛṣṭi*** view, point of view, opinion; vision.

**Durgā** ('the one who is difficult to approach') one of the many names or forms of the Goddess, this one being a ferocious one, said to have been created (or evoked) by the gods to rid themselves of Mahiṣāsura, the buffalo-demon, a usurper of their position and their oppressor. She killed him and thereby earned for herself the name Mahiṣāsuramardinī.

**Durgāpūjā** (also: Mahānavamī; cf. Daśahrā) a festival which is celebrated from the first till the ninth day of the bright half of the month Āśvina (September/October), in most parts of India, but particularly in Bengal. It commemorates the victory of Durgā over the buffalo-demon Mahiṣāsura and it culminates on the tenth day in a procession at the end of which the goddess is immersed in a river or in the sea.

**Dussehra** see Daśahrā.

***dvaita*** duality.

**Dvaitādvaita** see Bhedābheda.

**Dvaita Vedānta** the school of thought based on the teachings of Madhva which is called dualistic, because it recognizes the eternal existence of the absolute dimension of the divine on the one hand and of the relative material sphere of existence on the other. It is a further development of the philosophy of Rāmānuja in total opposition to Śaṅkara's Advaita Vedānta. The school recognizes *brahman* as the Absolute and identifies it with the Supreme Lord, God Viṣṇu. The world was created by God out of matter, a kind of subtle substance which is eternal. Individual selves ('souls') are also eternal and retain their separate, albeit God-dependent, existence even in the state of salvation which is granted as God's grace, but only to those who live pure lives. The best path to God is *bhaktimārga*. Those who do not turn to a pure life and to God may transmigrate in *saṁsāra* for ever. Those who in the pursuit of selfish aims commit evil may reach a point past redemption and face eternal damnation in infinite remoteness from God. (This and some other features of the teachings of this school are regarded as influenced by Christian theology.)

***dvāpara*** uncertainty, suspense; the side of the die marked with two points.

**Dvāpara Yuga** the third age within a *mahāyuga* according to Purāṇic world history, lasting 824,000 years. It corresponds to the heroic (copper or bronze) age of ancient Gr. mythology.

**Dvārakā**, also: Dvāravatī ('of many gates') the legendary capital of Kṛṣṇa's kingdom in Gujarat. The old town is supposed to have been on a sea cliff later claimed by the sea.

***dvija*** twice-born; an initiated member of one of the three higher castes.

***dvīpa*** island; continent. The Purāṇic mythical geography has several versions. One of them envisages seven continents surrounding Mount Meru like lotus leaves, themselves surrounded by seas. India, called Jambudvīpa, is one of them or is situated on the southern tip of a big continent so called.

**Dyaus Pitar** (*dyu*: sky, heaven; *pitar*: father; cf. Gr. Zeus Pater and Lat. Ju-piter) 'heavenly father', the originator of the world, together with the Earth mother (Pṛthivī Mātar) Before their separation they represented the primeval unity, Dyāvāpṛthivī. This is a version of one of several creation myths which existed in IE and Vedic antiquity.

***eka*** one; *ekatva*: oneness; cf. *tad ekam* of RV 10,129, where it means the primordial oneness prior to manifestation.

**Ekadanta** ('with one tusk') a name of Gaṇeśa.

***ekavrātya*** a solitary (accomplished) Vrātya wanderer.

**Ekavrātya** the highest cosmic being or deity of the Vrātya tradition known from the AV.

**Elements** (*bhūtas*) dynamic cosmic forces which, according to most Indian schools of thought, constitute the material universe and its phenomena, often called the 'great elements' (*mahābhūtas*). The theory of four or five elements is of IE origin and was known in European antiquity and recognized virtually up to the birth of modern chemistry and physics. Some systems developed quite sophisticated interpretations of their nature and function. The usual four elements are *pṛthivī* (earth, solidity), *āpas* (water, fluidity), *vāyu* (air, vibration) and *agni* (fire, heat, light), the additional fifth one being *ākāśa* (space, ether).

**Elephanta** an island off the coast of Bombay with an important Śivaistic rock-carved temple dated cca 450–750 A.D., possibly constructed under the patronage of the Rāṣṭrakūta dynasty.

**Ellorā, Elūrā** an important site of rock-carved shrines and cave temples near Aurangabad dated around the eighth century A.D. There are twelve Mahāyāna Buddhist caves, seventeen Hindu caves and a huge monolithic Śiva temple called Kailāśanātha carved out of a hillside. Later five Jain cave temples dated between the eighth and thirteenth centuries were added.

**Evolution** in the sense of a steady progress from lower stages to perfection is not a concept envisaged in Indian thought. All evolution is, so to speak, circular and proceeds in constant ups and downs rather than in an upward line. Having reached its evolutionary peak, the universe begins to deteriorate and eventually collapses before starting to evolve again. The same goes for civilizations and individuals in their successive lives. It is only by conscious decision and consistent effort that individual perfection can be achieved.

**Fakir** (fr. Arab. *faqir*, 'pauper') a Muslim ascetic or saint; a wandering wonder-maker or snake-charmer. In keeping with the all-inclusive tendencies of Hinduism, Islamic saints of repute and their graves attract recognition and reverence on the part of Hindus, often more so than in their own fold where some of them may appear to be heretics, because influenced by Hindu practices.

**Fate** as a concept of inevitable destiny has no place in the systems of Hindu thought. Generally speaking, the laws of *karma* are not agents influencing the life of the individual and of groups in a particular way, but channels through which actions produce their respective results. By modifying one's actions one can modify one's 'fate', not only in the future, but to a degree also in present events, although the consequences of past deeds cannot be entirely escaped. But there is no justification for regarding, as is sometimes done, the belief in the inevitability of karmic retribution as fatalism, since even though present consequences of past deeds cannot be avoided, there is always, in the Hindu outlook, the possibility of shaping one's future karmic destiny by considered actions in the present.

**Festivals** in Hinduism are many and of great importance, some of them deriving from IE antiquity, especially those associated with seasonal festivities. The most widely observed ones are Dīvālī, Daśahrā (Dusschra) or Durgāpūjā, Gaṇeśacaturthī, Holī and Śivarātri.

**Fire** was the main focus in Brahminic ritual. Usually three or five fires were set up for a sacrifice in the open. In the domestic ritual it was one fire which was kindled at the marriage ceremony and then continually maintained and used in sacrificial offerings. Ritual use of fire declined somewhat with the virtual abandonment of animal sacrifices. Cf. Agni.

**Five M's** a Tantric ritual procedure. See *pañcamākāra* and Tantrism.

**Freedom of will** is an implicit feature of the doctrine of karmic retribution which presupposes responsibility for one's thoughts, words and deeds and the capability to choose. The choice in terms of concrete action may be limited by circumstances brought about karmically, i.e. by one's own doing in the past, but this does not change the moral dilemma or affect the ability to choose what is perceived as good or at least to abstain from evil. The perception may, of course, be faulty and the individual 'pays' also for his mistakes. Therefore in the last analysis, consistent with the outlook of Hindu philosophy, the question of freedom of will is primarily the question of the search for knowledge, i.e. of choosing to search for truth, of neglecting it out of idleness or of rejecting it for immediate gain, while suppressing the thought of long-term effects. The situation of one who does not have at least a basic understanding of karmic laws or does not believe in them or has no knowledge of them equals the state of deepest ignorance conducive to wrong choices with detrimental consequences for his future lives.

**Fundamentalism** the belief in the literal truth of the scriptural sources of one's religion. In the absence of a central authority which could decree literal understanding of scriptures and in the face of the more or less general acceptance of different levels of interpretation of scriptural sources in Hinduism, fundamentalism has had little ground within it and occurs in a minor way only in some sectarian movements, e.g. with respect to the legends about Kṛṣṇa's life, but without any significant impact on the general trend of symbolical interpretations of scriptural materials.

**Funeral ceremonies** (*antyeṣṭi*) consist of a procession to the burning ground followed by cremation to the accompaniment of the recitation of sacred texts and by the circumambulation of the funeral pyre anti-clockwise. Charred bones are thrown into the river, traditionally on the third day. Libations and offerings (*piṇḍa*) for the dead follow for ten days.

***gadā*** mace, club, an ancient favourite weapon in battles.

**Gadādevī** Viṣṇu's mace depicted as a goddess.

**Gajendra** the king of elephants.

***gaṇa*** troop, host; used mainly for groups of deities when they appear together, e.g. Ādityas, or of lower deities in the retinue of high gods.

**Gaṇapati** another name of Gaṇeśa, the lord of Śiva's retinue.

***gandharva*** a lower male deity, usually fulfilling the function of a heavenly musician (female counterpart: *apsaras*); a spirit-being (ready to be reborn on earth).

**Gāndhī, Mohandās Karamchand** (1869–1948) the 'father' of India, who contributed enormously to the demise of the colonial rule in India. Having studied law in London and practised it in South Africa, he turned, on his return to India in 1915, to political activity, advocating *sanātana dharma* both in public and in his personal life. He accepted many formal and historical features of the Hindu tradition, such as reverence for the cow and the principle of the caste system – with modifications, particularly in that he rejected the limitations imposed on the untouchables, whom he called Harijans (children of God). He fought, without lasting success, for their integration into Hindu society. He further endorsed the doctrine of divine incarnations and also counted among *avatāras* the great figures of other religions, e.g. Jesus, whose Sermon on the Mount he greatly admired. He was also influenced by the ideas of a number of Western authors, e.g. Max Müller, Tolstoy, Ruskin and Thoreau, and combined them with ideas from the BhG (which, incidentally, he first read in Sir Edwin Arnold's translation). He was against the industrialization of India, canvassing for a return to simple rural life for the masses and for the renewal of home industries. One of his most powerful weapons in the fight for India's freedom from colonial rule was fasting when in prison which, invariably, made the British administration give in and release him for fear that he might die in prison. He used the weapon of a 'fast unto death' successfully also after the independence of India and its partition in order to stop Hindu pogroms taking place against Muslims in the republic, particularly in Calcutta and Delhi, in retaliation for Muslim atrocities against Hindus in Pakistan. This stance of his was resented by Hindu extremists and he was assassinated by one of them while he was on his way to his regular evening prayer meeting on 30.1.1948. India generally acknowledges her indebtedness to him, but does not follow his ideas.

**Gaṇeśa** the elephant-headed, pot-bellied god of wisdom and remover of obstacles who is in charge of a host of lower deities in the retinue of Śiva. His mount is a rat (*ākhu*) and he is very fond of sweetmeats. He is a son of Pārvatī, born from parings of her skin and only reluctantly adopted by Śiva. Clearly of non-Vedic origin, he emerged in the period of transition from Brāhmanism to Hinduism from the pre-Āryan trends of popular veneration of the elephant (with recognizable Harappan roots and also later Buddhist associations) and came to prominence in late Purāṇic times. His sectarian followers (Gāṇapatyas) regard him as the representation of the unmanifest source of reality from which emerged the manifested universe. This is expressed symbolically in his iconography by a bowl filled with sweetmeat balls (*modakas*), which represent world systems. A peculiar creation myth was invented for him: once, having stuffed his belly with sweetmeat balls, he was riding on his rat when it suddenly jumped, frightened by a snake. Gaṇeśa fell off, his belly burst open and the sweetmeat balls rolled out, whereupon he put them back again and repaired his belly by using the snake as a belt. In this 'myth' he, or his belly, represents the transcendental divine source, the snake the infinite cyclic movement of time (a clear allusion to Viṣṇu's snake Śeśa/Ananta), the scattering of the sweetmeat balls from his burst belly represents obviously the emanation of the world systems from the divine source and the act of collecting the balls and stuffing them back into his belly stands for the reabsorption of the worlds into the divine. Gaṇeśa also has a role in a particular Tantric path to liberation.

**Gaṇeśacaturthī** the festival celebrating Gaṇeśa's birthday on the fourth day of the bright half of the lunar month Bhādrapada (August/September). It is very popular and was proclaimed by Tilak as the universal festival of Hinduism, binding together the whole Hindu community.

**Gaṅgā** the most sacred river of Hinduism which is said to flow out of Viṣṇu's toe and descends to earth via Śiva's matted locks; as goddess she is the daughter of Himavat and sister of Umā.

***garbhagṛha*** ('womb-house') the inner sanctuary of Hindu temples, symbolically the birth-place of the universe and the meeting place of gods and men (the threshold between the transcendental and the phenomenal worlds).

***garuḍa*** a class of bird-like mythological beings, sometimes wrongly called eagles.

**Garuḍa** Viṣṇu's mount and the king of birds.

**Gauḍapāda** (cca 725 A.D.) the author of Māṇḍūkya Kārikā, an important work expounding the doctrine of Advaita Vedānta. The tradition has it that he was the teacher of Govindapāda who was the *guru* of Śaṅkara.

**Gayā** one of the seven sacred cities of Hinduism (in Bihār) and a place of pilgrimage, particularly for the followers of Viṣṇu. Nearby is the place, now known as Bodh-Gayā, where Siddhattha Gotama reached enlightenment and became the Buddha.

***gāyatrī*** a Vedic metre of twenty-four syllables; as goddess, Gāyatrī is a wife of Brahma and the mother of the four Vedas.

**Gāyatrī Mantra** the name of a verse in the RV (3,62,10) addressing the sun as Savitar ('vivifier') and hence known also as Sāvitrī Mantra. It is recited at the daily *pūjā* at dawn and dusk by all faithful brahmins: '*Oṁ, tat savitur vareṇyaṁ bhargo devasya dhīmahi dhiyo yo naḥ pracodayāt, oṁ.*' (We contemplate the glorious splendour of the divine Vivifier; may he enlighten our minds!)

***ghaṇṭā*** a hand-held bell used in rituals, both Hindu and Buddhist.

***ghāt*** (vern.; Skt.; *ghaṭṭa*) a bathing-place with steps leading into a river or pond, used for religious purposes; also: a place on the bank of a river with enough flowing water, used for cremation ('burning *ghāṭ*') and funeral rites, the relics and ashes being thrown into the river at the conclusion.

***ghee*** (vern.; Skt. *ghṛta*) melted butter, used frequently in religious offerings.

**Gheranda Saṁhitā** a textbook of Hatha Yoga, probably from the seventeenth century, heavily dependent on *Haṭhayoga-pradīpika*.

***Gītā Govinda*** a poetical work by Jayadeva (twelfth–thirteenth century) on the erotic exploits of Kṛṣṇa with Rādhā and other *gopīs*, often interpreted as a mystical allegory.

**God** there is no single expression in the Hindu tradition which would convey clearly the idea of one omnipotent divine being, as there is in the so-called monotheistic religions stemming from the Judeo-Christian-Islamic traditions. The designation *deva*, god, is applied in Hinduism both to the highest being in the universe, the

Supreme Lord, as well as to a large number of higher beings in his retinue or subordinate to him. But not even the Supreme Lord can claim all the attributes ascribed to the God of the Judeo-Christian-Islamic traditions. Yet the label of polytheism which has been attached by some European scholars to the whole of the Vedic-Brahminic-Hindu tradition is hardly appropriate, being too simplistic and misleading, because it does not convey the deep and sophisticated background of this tradition. Right from Vedic times onwards it envisaged the source of manifested reality and of its inhabitants to be a divine, intelligent and transcendental oneness or unity whose nature is that of an infinite personality (*puruṣa*, RV 10,90) which manifests itself only partially as phenomenal reality or the world, and for the purpose of 'creating' it uses its forces or 'potencies' which appear to humans as separate divine agents, beings or gods: 'What is one the sages call by many names' (RV 1,164,46). Thus these forces or gods are not much more than, for example, the angels, archangels and other higher beings of the Judeo-Christian heavenly hierarchy, some of whom are also known by their personal names and the tasks they are said to have performed in world history. Later, Hindu tradition refers to the one true God as *īśvara*, the Lord, never losing sight of the fact, however, that he also has a 'bigger' transcendental dimension which is not conceivable by the limited human mind: this is the Upaniṣadic *brahman* of whom the god 'creator' Brahma is the first and highest manifestation. When the status of Lordship is ascribed to Viṣṇu, or Śiva or any other deity by sectarian followers, this hidden dimension is always understood as underlying them, while the other *devas* are seen as being subordinate to the Lord. Another development of Hindu theology led to the formation of the concept of the divine Trinity, representing different aspects of one reality. See Trimūrti.

**Gods** (*devas*) in Hinduism are, generally speaking (leaving aside sophisticated philosophical interpretations), higher beings with long life-spans who are not, however, exempt from the laws of the cosmos. They are born in their heavenly worlds as a result of their karmic merits and may subsequently be born as humans or in lower worlds just as humans may reach heavenly birth as gods if they develop their minds accordingly and deserve it as a result of their actions. In popular Hinduism gods are important concrete symbols of the divine as well as cosmic intelligences and divine personages in their own right, usually with a specific area of influence. They are worthy of worship and offerings and capable of granting boons. They figure in many mythological stories and are represented in effigies with many symbolical attributes which express their character and domain.

**Gopāla** (cowherd) the name of the young Kṛṣṇa.

***gopī*** milkmaid, 'cowherdess'; symbolically; the human 'soul' in the *bhakti* relationship to God. In the legend of Kṛṣṇa the maidens and women of the pastoral communities of Vṛdavān were charmed by him, fell madly in love with him and ran after him whenever he played his flute. This is supposed to indicate the overpowering depth of the *bhakta*'s love for God. On another level they are regarded as multiple representations of *śakti*.

***gopura*** the gate-tower leading into the courtyard of South Indian temples. It developed into a much larger construction than the central tower over the sanctum. There are usually four of them.

**Gorakhnath** (Skt. Gorakṣanātha) the second human *guru* of the Nātha yoga cult (possibly of twelfth or thirteenth century), reputed to have been a *siddha*. The invention of the Hatha Yoga system is ascribed to him and he is also credited with the founding of the Kāṇphaṭa order of yogis (Gorakhnāthis) and with the authorship of a work on Hatha Yoga called *Gorakṣaśataka*. The first human *guru* was Matsyendranath.

**Gosvāmin** a title of the theologians of the sectarian movement in the tradition of Caitanya. There were six of them and they wrote over two hundred Sanskrit works, maintaining that Kṛṣṇa was not an *avatāra* of God, but the Supreme God himself.

***gotra*** clan.

**Govinda** (cow-keeper, chief herdsman) a name of Kṛṣṇa.

**Grace** an ambiguous notion, not easily defined, but current in theistic religions, some of which insist that salvation cannot be secured by the individual's effort, but is possible only as a result of God's grace, sometimes even bestowed exclusively on specially 'chosen ones'. There is no precise equivalent of the term 'grace' in the Hindu tradition. Generally speaking, Hindu religious philosophy requires the fulfilment of certain conditions for gaining salvation, among them determination to find truth, dedication to the goal and constantly renewed effort on the path to it. Help is of course needed in terms of instruction and encouragement by an experienced teacher backed by a body of doctrinal tradition and tried methods, and in the case of the religiously-minded by scriptures, believed to be revealed or inspired. In sectarian circles centred round the worship of a personal God (e.g. Kashmiri Trika, Vallabha or Śaiva Siddhānta) divine assistance is sought, hoped for or expected and sometimes even regarded as essential. Various expressions are used, such as *karuṇā* (basic meaning 'compassion'), *prasāda* (favour, kindness) or *varada* (granting a boon). But no expression current in the sources of Hinduism is consistent with the idea of salvation granted to the believer in the sense of an 'unmerited gift of God' without his own effort, his dedication to a path to God or his commitment to pure living or some other active contribution on his part.

***grāmadevatā*** ('village deity') an effigy guarding the village against evil influences, usually installed on its outskirts in a simple shrine or in the open. It may sometimes be a deity of negative disposition, regarded as malevolent but sufficiently propitiated by the villagers to frighten away only intruders. Cases have been recorded of effigies of British tax collectors installed in this capacity.

***gṛhastha*** householder; *gṛhasthya* – the second stage of the system of *āśrama dharma.*

**Gṛhya Sūtras** a set of rules for domestic rituals.

***guhyaka*** a class of goblin, half bird and half horse, in the retinue of Kubera. They guard his hidden treasures.

***guṇa*** cord, string; attribute, quality; the three *guṇas* (*sattva*, *rajas* and *tamas*, i.e. purity, energy and inertia) of the Sāṅkhya teachings are forces of nature (*prakṛti*) which figure also in several other post-classical systems and in popular religious thought.

**Gupta** the name of a dynasty which ruled during the Golden Age of Indian civilization (cca A.D. 320–510). It represents the peak of Buddhist, Hindu and Jain artistic development in sculpture and architecture as well as cave painting (see Ajantā). One of the finest examples of Hindu sculpture of this period is Viṣṇu Anantaśāyin on the south wall of the Daśāvatāra Temple in Deogarh.

***guru*** teacher; spiritual guide; spiritual head of a Hindu sect or community. The institution of *gurus* is an important feature of the Hindu tradition and is entirely separate from the institution of hereditary priesthood. In some sects and schools of yoga practice unquestioning obedience to its *guru* is required, in others the attitudes may be less strict and at the other end of the spectrum his status may resemble that of a benevolent teacher or adviser, but great respect or reverence is always due to him. Most Hindus do not belong to any particular sect, school of spiritual practice or *āśram*, but they usually have a personal *guru*, who need not belong to the same caste and need not even be a Hindu, to guide or advise them not only on spiritual and religious matters, but also on practical matters in family life and on personal problems.

**Halāhala** the name of a deadly poison, one of the by-products of the churning of the cosmic ocean by the gods and titans in their effort to obtain the drink of immortality. The poison threatened to destroy all life, but was drunk by Śiva who, as the great Yogi, was already immortal, and so he could thereby save the world. (This feat is already alluded to in the RV 10,136 and is an early reference to the notion of the task of salvation which a god, or God, can take on himself.)

***haṁsa*** goose, swan; symbol of spiritual achievement; honorific title suggesting such an achievement.

**Haṁsa Mantra** *so'ham* ('I am He'). It asserts the inmost identity of God and man. Quick repetition of this *mantra* makes it sound like *haṁso* (which is the nominative of *haṁsa*), hence its name.

**Hanumān** the chief of the monkey tribe which helped prince Rāma to recover his wife Sītā, abducted to Laṅkā by its demon-king Rāvaṇa. Hanumān then obtained the status of a god.

**Hara** a name of Śiva.

**Harappan civilization**, also known as Mohenjo-daro or the Indus valley civilization, flourished between 3000–1900 B.C. and is known only from archaeological excavations. Suffering from internal decline towards the end, it was finished off as a result of the Āryan immigration. Many of its religious phenomena later reappeared in Hinduism, e.g. the worship of the Great Mother, the so-called proto-Śiva in his aspect as Yogapati and Paśupati, the *liṅga-yoni* cult, the worship of tree deities etc.

**Hardwār** see Haridvāra.

**Hare Krishna movement** a popular designation for the International Society for Kṛṣṇa Consciousness (ISKCON) which was founded by Svāmi Bhaktivedānta Prabhupāda (1896–1977) in 1966 as a modern off-shoot of the *bhakti* tradition of Caitanya.

**Harem** (fr. Arab. *haram*, 'prohibited'; Skt. *antaḥpura*, inner quarter) a secluded part within a household reserved for women. In earlier times only the upper classes and particularly kings observed certain rules which limited to some extent the contact of their womenfolk with the outer world. These rules were later tightened under the influence of Islam, but never to the same extent as in Muslim households.

**Hari** a name of Viṣṇu.

**Haridvāra** ('Viṣṇu's gate'), Hardwar one of the seven sacred cities of Hinduism and a place of pilgrimage, at the spot where Gaṅgā leaves the mountains for the North Indian plains. It is also one of the four places where some drops of the nectar of immortality fell when gods and demons were fighting over it, an event commemorated by a Kuṁbha Mela once in twelve years.

**Harihara** the combined name of Viṣṇu and Śiva. It is used to indicate the essential unity of the two and, in general, the underlying non-sectarian Hindu philosophy asserting that the divine is one, although it takes on many forms and names.

**Harihara Mūrti** a composite image of the twin deity. Its right half represents Śiva and symbolizes time and its left half which represents Viṣṇu is in his female form (as Mohinī) and symbolizes space. Thus the effigy stands for the temporary manifestation of the universe in space.

**Harijan** ('born of God'; child of God) an expression coined by Gāndhī for the untouchables, now officially termed the 'scheduled classes', whom he wanted to be fully integrated into Hindu society, a dream yet to come true.

**Hārītī** Kubera's wife depicted usually with one or more children.

**Harṣa** (Harṣavardhana, 606–646/7) the last great Hindu ruler in India before the Islamic conquests, descended from the Guptas on his mother's side, who consolidated North India after the Hun invasions and ruled from Kanauj, patronizing Buddhism and emulating Aśoka. A great patron of the arts, he himself wrote dramatic works some of which have been preserved.

**Hatha Yoga,** *haṭhayoga* a system of physical and breathing exercises aimed at developing a perfect body as the basis for further spiritual progress to be achieved through Kuṇḍalinī Yoga. Its legendary founder was Gorakhnath.

***Haṭhayogapradīpikā*** ('a Lamp for Hatha Yoga') a work by Svātmārāma (cca fifteenth century) expounding the techniques of Hatha Yoga and partly also of Kuṇḍalinī Yoga. It is based on an earlier work by Gorakhnāth called *Gorakṣaśataka.*

**Himālaya** ('the abode of the snow') in popular mythology regarded as the abode of the gods, it denotes not only the actual mountain range, but also the invisible higher and subtle spiritual realms whose centre is the mythical Mount Meru.

**Himavat** god of the 'snow-covered mountains' (Himālayas) and the father of Pārvatī, the wife of Śiva.

**Hindu** as adj.: of Indian religion, belonging to Hinduism; as noun: a devotee or follower of Hinduism. It is the Av. and Persian equivalent of Skt. *sindhu* (river, as in Saptasindhu; also meaning: great water, sea, ocean). It was used in Persia to denote the land and people beyond the great expanse of water (i.e. the river later called Indus, the latinized form of the word *sindhu*). After their conquest of Persia it was adopted by the Muslims for the subcontinent and also to refer to the religion of India. The latter meaning came to be recognized by the Hindus themselves and has gained general acceptance. In the absence of formal registers of members such as have been developed in Christian denominations, it has never been easy to decide who is a Hindu. Until comparatively recently it could be said that whoever was born within a Hindu community, conformed to caste regulations and accepted the Veda as his sacred scripture was a Hindu. On those grounds the Buddha could not be regarded as one, and Buddhism developed into a new religion. The high spiritual content of the Buddha's message and his stature, however, later led the Brahminic orthodoxy to include him in the system of Hinduism as a divine incarnation, albeit with some distortions. In modern times the perception of who is or can be a Hindu has broadened as a result of innovations brought about by various reform movements, prompted by the encounter of Hinduism with European civilization. Thus castes can no longer be viewed as an integral part of Hinduism as a religion, and although they persist as a social prejudice, accepting their regulations is no longer a condition of being a Hindu. Birth also lost its importance as a criterion for being a Hindu so that assimilation, e.g. by marriage, is possible, and 'conversion' is no longer an impossibility, despite the reluctance of some orthodox sections to accept it. Another modern development has been a revaluation of Hinduism with an emphasis on its essence as a spiritual and universalistic teaching. In that light, belief in the Veda need not mean its literal acceptance as divine revelation: it may be replaced by acknowledgment of the inspired nature of its spiritual message. The criterion of who is a Hindu could thus be based also on a person's acceptance of the world view expressed by the concept of Sanātana Dharma. Even so, generally speaking, whoever follows some traditional form of Hindu practice or worship on whatever level has to be regarded for all practical purposes as a Hindu, however limited might be his understanding of the concept of Sanātana Dharma or his ability to articulate it.

**Hinduism** the designation for the mainstream religion of the Indian people. The term was coined by European scholars and came to be generally accepted in India and throughout the world.

**Hiraṇyagarbha** the cosmic 'golden egg' which floated in space on the ethereal ocean for a year, then parted in two halves, forming heaven and earth. The god Brahma as creator was born out of it. This is one of several Vedic cosmogonic myths.

**Hiraṇyakaśipu** ('golden-robed') the demon-king killed by Viṣṇu in his incarnation as Narasiṁha.

**Holī** (Holākā, Holikā) a very popular spring festival celebrated on the last, i.e. full moon, day of the lunar month Phālguna (February/March), by jumping over bonfires on the preceding night and on the day itself by people throwing coloured water at each other and with games, including various forms of licentious behaviour. Many of its features point to its ancient, prehistoric origin. In some parts of India it is associated with Kṛṣṇa's dalliances with the *gopīs*.

***homa*** oblation, offering of *ghee* to fire.

***hotar*** (cf. Av. *zaotar*) a RV brahmin, the chief priest who recites the hymns from the RV during Vedic rituals.

***iḍā*** in the RV it usually means a libation of milk or a food offering; in Kuṇḍalinī Yoga *iḍā nāḍī* is the left channel in the subtle body parallel to the spine, conducting *prāṇa*.

**Ilāhābād (Allāhābād)** see Prayāga.

**Image worship**, sometimes still strongly referred to as idol worship or idolatry, is best explained on the basis of the Pañcarātra theory of five types of Viṣṇu's self-revelation. These are: (1) as the Supreme Reality; (2) as his emanations (*vyūhas*); (3) as his incarnations (*avatāras*); (4) as the inner controller (*antaryāmi*) of all selves; and (5) as images or representations of himself. The image is thus explained as being virtually on a par with all his other aspects and it is therefore an effective vehicle for the realization by the worshipper of Viṣṇu's aspect as the Supreme Reality.

**Indirā** a name of Lakṣmī.

**Indo-Āryan** the designation for the IE tribes whose languages belong to the philological group of which the classical representative is Sanskrit. They are now spoken mainly in India (as Hindi, Bengali, Pañjābi, Gujarāti etc.), but in their early form were spoken by the Proto-Indo-Āryan tribes when they still lived in Iran, and before that in Central Asia. (Some differences in spoken language probably existed among Indo-Āryan tribes even earlier when they still lived in Eastern Europe.) One Indo-Āryan language still spoken in Central Asia (called Parya and close to Hindi and Pañjābi) was discovered only in the mid 1950s in Tadjikistan and Uzbekistan (formerly in the Soviet Union). Obviously, the ancestors of its present speakers had never made it in ancient times to Iran and India with the other Indo-Āryan tribes.

**Indo-European** (IE) the designation for the family of nations who speak languages which show certain common features in the structure of their grammar and in vocabulary as well as some traces of a culture which they once shared. It includes all European languages (except Finnish, Estonian, Hungarian and Basque) and their early forms and predecessors, including classical Greek and Latin, as well as the Iranian group and the Sanskrit-related (Indo-Āryan) languages. The prehistoric ancestral home of all these peoples is thought to have been in Southern Russia, from where they migrated in the course of several millennia to their present abodes in India, parts of the Middle East and all over Europe (and then all over the world through modern colonial expansion).

**Indo-Iranian** the designation for the two closely related IE groups, the Indo-Āryan and the Iranian, the latter comprising also the ancient language of Avesta as well as the Afghan and Persian groups, together with some other languages scattered from the Caspian Sea to Central Asia such as Tadjik and Kurdish. It is assumed that Indo-Āryan and Iranian once formed a single group, but that the split occurred or started occurring already in Europe before their migration eastwards.

**Indra** originally an important Vedic god who acted as the main agent of several creation myths. The most important one among them is the myth of IE origin which describes creation as his combat with the serpent-demon or dragon Vṛtra whom he pierced with his spear, thereby releasing waters, or rescuing captive maidens, symbolizing the powers of creation (cf. the Gr. myths of Perseus and Andromeda and of Theseus and Ariadne, and tales from European folklore about the knight in shining armour rescuing the princess from a dragon, and the legend of St. George). In another creation myth Indra is described as separating the heaven and earth and propping them up with his spear to keep them apart. Indra was furthermore the main god of the Āryan warriors during their conquest of North India and appears also as the king of the lower heaven of 'Thirty-three gods'. (For his efforts to discover the nature of his true self see Virocana.) On the popular level in later Hinduism he is mostly regarded as the rain god (a function which was performed in Vedic times by Parjaṇya). He is seen, in this context, as killing the demon Vṛtra, who is here represented by monsoon clouds, with his spear (lightning), thereby releasing the life-giving waters. He is served by the white elephant Airāvata as his mount.

**Indra-khīla** Indra's post, a pillar placed in ancient times at the city gate for protection. It is a symbol of the axis of the world which connects all levels of reality, from the material one up to the spiritual, and when installed, it puts the city into the wider cosmic context.

**Indrāṇī** the wife of Indra and one of the seven mother goddesses (*saptamātṛkās*).

**Indraprastha**, vern. Indapat the capital of the kingdom of the Pāṇḍavas, one of the two warring parties in the Mhb, now in the area of Old Delhi.

***indriya*** sense; sense organ.

***indu*** drop; sacred drop, a drop of *soma*; the moon.

**Integral Yoga** a term coined by Aurobindo for his notion of a global path to the realization of the Divine. It envisages the spiritualization of the whole universe through comprehensive Yoga practice in the context of living within a spiritually minded, goal-directed community – an élite which, if large enough and genuine, can bring about the uplifting of the rest.

**International Society for Kṛṣṇa Consciousness** (ISKCON, popularly known as 'Hare Krishna' movement) a modern sectarian movement with a firm organizational structure founded in 1966 by Svāmi Bhaktivedānta Prabhupāda (1896–1977) within the mainstream Hindu *bhakti* tradition influenced by Caitanya and centred around the cult of Kṛṣṇa as the Lord. Besides its activities based in India and its aim to serve emigrant Hindu communities, it has a strong missionary drive directed towards other nationals, an innovation within the Hindu tradition. It now has temples and semi-monastic communities in many Western countries.

***īśa, īśvara*** the Lord; in sectarian movements it is the title of the creator and ruler of the universe.

***īśvarapraṇidhāna*** total surrender to the Lord. As one of the *niyamas* in Patañjali's *aṣṭaṅga yoga*, it can be interpreted as the surrender of the self in the process of yoga training without necessarily referring to a personal god.

***iṣṭadevatā*** the chosen deity to whom a believer owes his sole or main allegiance; a chosen or favourite concrete form or image (*mūrti*) of a deity under which a Hindu formally worships God or the ultimate reality; a preferred deity whom a Hindu chooses as a concrete and approachable symbol of the inexpressible and transcendental divine Absolute (*brahman*) for the purposes of meditation as required by certain techniques of yoga.

***itihāsa*** (Skt. *iti ha āsa*=so it was) story, history; originally a term for tales and legends excluded from the Vedas (but sometimes called the fifth Veda), later applied also to works of heroic history and to legendary literature such as the two great epics and also the Purāṇas. Although not regarded as divine revelations, these writings are crucially important in Hinduism as sources of religious teachings accessible to all.

**Jagadguru** ('world teacher') a title used by some sectarian leaders, e.g. in the South Indian Lingāyata movement.

**Jagannātha** the 'Lord of the world'. It is the name of a crude effigy without limbs and with big painted eyes, housed in the temple of Puri, now regarded as a particular manifestation of Viṣṇu (or Kṛṣṇa). It is buried and newly carved in a twelve-year cycle. An annual festival is held in the month of Aṣāḍha (June/July) when the deity is taken out in a procession on a heavy car with huge wheels, to which early English observers mistakenly applied the name of the deity, which then entered English vocabulary as 'juggernaut' (a heavy vehicle or lorry). The deaths that have taken place under its wheels have been mostly accidents in the crowded conditions, rather than ritual suicides as was alleged in the reports of missionaries in the last century. It appears that originally the effigy was an aniconic representation of god in the form of a wooden post among the Savaras, the aborigines of Orissa, and it evolved into the present figure when it came to be appropriated by the Hindu cult. The Saravas still retain the right to carve the new effigy each time it is replaced and the brahmins only paint the eyes.

**Jainism** a religious tradition made important by Vardhamāna, a contemporary of the Buddha, who adopted the title Jina (victor) on attaining spiritual accomplishment. He is regarded as the twenty-fourth and last *tīrthaṅkara* ('ford-maker', i.e. one who enables others to cross the stream of *saṁsāra* to the other shore of liberation). The previous one, Pārśva, is a semihistorical personality of the seventh century B.C., the others are mythical. The teachings of Jainism overlap in some aspects with those of Buddhism, Sāṅkhya and Yoga and share some features with Hinduism, but reject the authority of the Vedas. Great importance is ascribed to *ahiṁsā*, which substantially influenced Hinduism. Hindus tend to worship in some Jain temples and visit Jain places of pilgrimage and brahmins sometimes officiate in them.

**Jalaśāyin** ('reposing on the waters') an epithet of Viṣṇu when resting afloat between world periods on the snake Ananta/Śeṣa. A famous effigy of him is in Budha Nilkantha in Nepal.

***jambu*** rose-apple, the fruit from the tree *Eugenia jambolana* (popularly: pear).

**Jambūdvīpa** the 'pear-shaped' island, the ancient name of the 'continent' of India.

**Jambuvṛkṣa** a tree, *Eugenia jambolana*, believed to be a wishing tree, reaching with its branches into the unseen world.

***japa*** repetition; 'murmuring meditation'; inward recitation of *mantras*.

***jaṭa*** matted hair as a sign of mourning; worn also by members of a particular sect of ascetics.

***jāti*** birth; birth into a certain clan; clan; subcaste.

**Jayadeva** (twelfth to thirteenth century) the author of *Gītā Govinda*, an influential Sanskrit poetical work about the love of Kṛṣṇa for Rādhā and other *gopīs*.

***jina*** conqueror, victor.

**Jina** a title given to those who have reached liberation, having conquered all obstacles. It is used mainly for Vardhamāna, the historical founder of Jainism, and only occasionally for the Buddha and others.

***jīva*** life; individual 'soul' in Jainism and some other non-Hindu systems; *jīvātman*: individual 'soul' or the individual aspect of the universal essence (*ātman*) which appears outwardly as a particular human personality endowed with an individual character, while at the same time being deep down one with the universal essence or pure *ātman*.

***jīvanmukta*** one who has reached liberation while still living in the world in his material body; *jīvanmukti*: the state of liberation achieved during one's lifetime.

***jñāna*** knowledge; in Vedāntic texts it usually designates insight or higher (direct) knowledge of reality. It is gained on the 'path of knowledge' (*jñānamārga*) by contemplation leading to an inner vision of the absolute truth.

**Jñānadeva**, also Jñāneśvara (cca 1275–96) a Marātha *bhakti* poet, mystic and philosopher with a Nātha background.

**Jñāna Yoga** a systematic spiritual discipline geared to acquiring direct insight knowledge, often presented in conjunction with the philosophical background of the Advaita Vedānta system of thought. It adopts many technical procedures of Patañjali's classical Yoga.

**Jumna** see Yamunā.

***jyotirlinga*** 'pillar of light', an aspect of Śiva

***jyotisa*** astronomy, astrology, one of the Vedāṅgas.

***ka*** who; sometimes used as an expression indicating the nameless source of the universe.

**Kabīr** (uncertain dates, possibly 1440–1518) a wandering saint of Hindu background with a theistic attitude of Vaiṣṇava type and with Sūfī sympathies. He was also influenced by the early form of South Indian Christianity (traditionally believed to have been brought to India by the apostle Thomas, but probably transmitted in early centuries to India via Persia). He promoted the spirit of harmony between Islam and Hinduism, but enlarged it to include non-Hindu religions also ('Allah and Rāma are only different names of the same reality.'). This was an attitude which was also to be embraced in modern times by Ramakrishna and Gāndhī. Kabīr discarded rituals and saw *bhakti* as the true road to salvation. His followers formed a sect (Kabīr Panthīs), still in existence. His teachings influenced Guru Nānak, the founder of Sikhism, and many of his sayings and poems are included in Ādi Granth, the sacred book of the Sikhs.

**Kailāsa** a mountain in the Himālayas in Tibet, sacred to Hindus who place there Śiva's paradise and the seat of Kuvera (Kubera), the god of riches.

***kaivalya*** 'aloneness'; complete autonomy from conditioned states of existence within the universe which are conjured up by *prakṛti*. It is the realization of the final freedom of the *puruṣa* or individual spirit in the Sāṅkhya system. The term is also used for the final state of purity in Classical Yoga and as the equivalent of liberation in various other movements.

***kāla*** as noun: time; fate, destiny; death; as adj.; black, dark blue.

**Kāla** the god of death; one of the names of Śiva and of Yama.

**Kāla Bhairava** a name of Śiva as destroyer.

***kāladaṇḍa*** the staff of death, the emblem of Yama.

**Kāladūta** the messenger of death.

***kālakūṭa*** deadly poison; one of the expressions applied to the poison churned out of the cosmic ocean, before the drink of immortality (*amṛta*) was obtained, by *devas* and *asuras* in a rare example of co-operation between them. It was drunk by Śiva to save the world from its destructive power and as a result, his throat became dark.

**Kālāmukha** a South Indian sect of the Pāśupata cult with Tantric connections. Its members wear a black mark on their foreheads.

**Kālanātha** the Lord of time, an epithet of Śiva.

***kalaśa*** waterpot. It is worn by one type of ascetic as a symbol of the universe (cf. Cosmic waters) and its generative power.

***kali*** the throw of dice with one dot; the loser; Kali Yuga: the fourth (present) age in the Purāṇic world history, often called the dark age, but the name is probably derived from the throw of dice. It started, according to Purāṇic reckoning, in 3102 B.C. with the mythical destructive battle on the Kurukṣetra described in the Mhb. Its duration is given as 432,000 years and its dawn, lasting one twentieth of its total duration, is to be relatively mild, with longer periods of peace, but its final stages will witness the complete breakdown of civilized forms of life and the total loss of spiritual and moral values which only a new divine incarnation (Kalki) will be able to remedy.

**Kāli** (the black one), often called Kāli Mā (mother) the most wrathful form of the Goddess who, according to some sects, requires human sacrifices. She represents the destructive aspect of 'mother' nature.

**Kālidāsa** regarded as the greatest Indian poet and author of dramas and dated around the reign of Chandra Gupta II Vikramaditya who ruled from cca 380–413. His best known work is the drama *Abhijñānaśakuntala* (The Recognition of Śakuntala) and his best love lyric is *Meghadūta* (Cloud Messenger).

**Kalki** the tenth major incarnation of Viṣṇu, who is expected to come at the end of Kali Yuga (riding a white horse which is sometimes represented with wings) to institute a new age of purity and spiritual renewal. He is sometimes regarded in neo-Hindu thought as a symbol of a future spiritual civilization (cf. Radhakrishnan's book *Kalki or the Future of Civilization*).

***kalpa*** a Brahma's day, a world period, in Purāṇic terms equal to a thousand *mahāyugas*, representing 4,320 million years.

***kāma*** desire, lust, pleasure, love; in the RV (10,129) it is a cosmic force or intelligence responsible for bringing about polarity within the primeval oneness and for starting the process of manifestation; as one of the *puruṣārthas* it has its place in the second stage of life, that of the householder, since it is then his *āśramadharma* or sacred duty to experience fulfilment in his own love life, as well as to see to the fulfilment of his partner(s).

**Kāma** god of love who carries a sugar-cane bow and pierces hearts with his arrows. His mount is a parrot. Appearing already in the Av., he is no doubt of IE lineage (cf. the Lat. Cupid and Gr. Eros).

**Kāmadhenu, Kāmaduh** the wishing-cow which emerged from the churning of the cosmic ocean.

**Kāma Sūtra** a treatise on love written by Vātsyāyana Mallanāga (fourth or fifth century A.D.). Profound understanding of erotic matters and skill in sexual love may be regarded as more or less a religious duty of a Hindu within the system of *āśrama dharma*, i.e. duties to be met according to the stage of life he is in. In the second stage of his life, as a householder, one of the two human aims (*puruṣārthas*) he ought to realize is *kāma* or sensory and aesthetic fulfilment on all levels which, of course, includes love in all its aspects.

**Kāmaśāstra** the name for the category of literature dealing with love and the techniques of love-making.

**Kāñcīpura** (Conjeevaram) one of the seven sacred cities of Hinduism, located in South India, with a famous temple.

**Kāṇphaṭa ('split ear') yogis** a sect of Śaiva ascetics, also known as Gorakhnātis, stressing the practice of Hatha Yoga and the acquisition of occult powers, outwardly distinguished by split ear-lobes and large earrings.

**Kanyā Kumārī** the 'virgin goddess', a form of Durgā worshipped particularly in her temple on the southernmost tip of India (Cape Comorin) as the 'goddess of bewitching beauty'.

**Kāpālika** a South Indian sect of the Pāśupata cult with Tantric connotations, worshipping Śiva Bhairava. Its ascetics carried a skull as a bowl for food.

***kāraṇa śarīra*** causal body, the carrier of karmic seeds into future lives. Cf. *liṅga śarīra*.

***karma, karman*** action, deed, ritual action, religious observance or duty; the cosmic law of balance effective in the sphere of morality (succeeding the Vedic notion of *ṛta*) which operates in this life and through successive lives as a kind of natural 'law of retribution' for human actions on the principle 'as you have sown so you will reap'.

***karmamārga*** the path of action, a way to salvation which, in its orthodox form based on Pūrva Mīmāṁsā, uses mainly ritual and in its more broadly based outlook stresses also moral action as a means for achieving spiritual progress.

**Karma Yoga** a spiritual path expounded by Kṛṣṇa in the BhG which uses consciously disinterested but considered action to enhance the chances of liberation.

**Kārttikeya**, also: Skanda and Kumara (in Tamil: Murugan) the god of war and disease, son of Śiva from his seed which he cast into fire. The ashes with his seed were then swept into Gaṅgā who brought him forth in due course. He is therefore also regarded as the son of Agni and of Gaṅgā and sometimes called Agnibhū and Gaṅgāja. But in another version Śiva begot him alone in his form as Ardhanārī. He was brought up by the Kṛttikās (Pleiades) and then adopted by Pārvatī. His mount is a peacock.

***karuṇā*** compassion in the sense of a meditative experience of universal suffering in Buddhism and Patañjali's system, in Hindu sources rarely used also in the sense of the 'grace of God'.

**Kāśī** the ancient name for Varāṇasī (Benares).

**Kathak** (story) a North Indian solo dance form with narrative contents, usually giving episodes from the life of Kṛṣṇa and Rādhā. It originated during the fifteenth or sixteenth century.

**Kathākali** (story-play) a mimetic dance drama which developed from the village pantomime in the fourteenth century in Malabār when taken up by court dancers. It conveys epic stories in which female parts are danced by young male dancers.

**Kauravas** descendants of Kuru, a prince of the Lunar dynasty, and one of the two warring parties in the Mhb.

***kavi*** poet, seer, sage.

***kāvya*** poem, poetry; poetics; '*kāvya* literature' usually refers to the court poetry of the classical age of Indian history in Gupta and immediately post-Gupta time (320–700 A.D.).

***kāya*** body; trunk of a tree.

***keśin*** the 'long-haired one', the solitary figure of a wandering accomplished sage, known mainly from the RV 10,136 and some other references, also in the AV. Unlike the *ṛṣis* who did not withdraw from society, but were engaged in guiding their communities and represented the mainstream of the Vedic tradition, *keśins* were outside it and from them there is a direct line to the phenomenon of *śramaṇas* and other types of ascetic from which later emerged Jainism and Buddhism and various types of yoga movements.

**Khajurāho** the temple capital of the Candella dynasty of Rājput origin, with Jain and Hindu temples from the tenth to eleventh centuries renowned for their erotic sculpture of high artistic quality.

**Kingship** an institution which was for a long time essential to the Hindu view of social order. It developed in the Āryan society in the aftermath of their conquest of India from the function of tribal chieftains and heads of clans who had risen to prominence when strong leadership was needed in wars. Their power increased with the strength of the warrior class which is reflected in the Purāṇic myth about Brahma appointing Indra as the king of the gods to lead them in the war with the demons. Even prior to that the head of the family, clan or tribe had a certain responsibility for orderly relations among those under his jurisdiction, and also for securing their welfare, besides by normal means, by his mediation with the gods, because he had also a priestly function (a feature which is still to a degree retained by heads of Hindu families). Chieftains and war leaders obtained their position by election or consensus and this is reflected in another Purāṇic myth in which people appealed to Brahma for a king to secure order in society and nature and promised in return to agree to taxes and other tributes as well as to the principle of his rule by *daṇḍa*. A residue of this relationship is still to some extent projected onto top politicians in India.

***kinnara*** a category of mythical beings in human form with horses' heads, dwelling in Kubera's paradise on Mount Kailāsa.

***kīrtan*(*a*)** 'singing the praises of God', usually in a devotional gathering.

***kīrtimukha*** a demon-mask placed above the door of Śiva's temples to drive away evil beings.

**Knowledge** (Skt. *vidyā*, *jñāna*, *samjñā*, *prajñā*) is usually defined in Hindu systems on two different levels, but the terminology is not unified and differs from school to school. Its use and meaning has to be ascertained from the context. Knowledge on a lower level, including learning based on the study of texts and mere hearing, although valuable in pointing one in the right direction, still counts as ignorance with respect to true reality and must be superseded by intuitive, visionary or direct perception of truth, resulting in higher knowledge, most often referred to as wisdom (*prajñā*).

**Konārak temple** (thirteenth century) formerly known as the 'Black Pagoda' (now cleaned up), it is dedicated to Sūrya, the sun god, and its main hall was built to represent his chariot. When in full glory it exceeded in size any Khajurāho temple and it also competes in artistic quality with Khajurāho's erotic sculpture, besides showing a number of dancing postures which helped in modern time in the renewal of the classical dance form Bharata Nāṭya.

***kośa*** vessel, cup, sheath; a Vedāntic term for successive layers forming the gross, subtle and causal bodies in the complex structure of the human personality.

**Krishnamurti, Jiddu** (1895–1986) was born in Madanapalle in South India as the eighth child of Brahmin parents. His father later worked, as a widowed retired civil servant, for the Theosophical Society in Adyār where in 1909 C. W. Leadbeater, a close associate of A. Besant, recognized in the boy a future spiritual leader. He was then educated in France and England and made the Head of the 'Order of the Star of the East' founded for him in 1911 as a vehicle for his future mission as a new world teacher and saviour of mankind. The name was shortened to the 'Order of the Star' in April 1927 when it was thought that the beginning of his world mission was imminent. But in August of the same year Krishnamurti rejected the role prepared for him, dissolved the 'Order of the Star of the East' and embarked on a career of an independent teacher of Truth which, he proclaimed, 'is a pathless land' and 'cannot be organized' and 'cannot be brought down' just as a mountain-top cannot be brought to the valley, 'rather the individual must make the effort to ascend it'. He had obviously realized the danger which lies in any kind of institutalization of a spiritual message. He also refused to be linked to any of the existing spiritual traditions. Yet despite this insistence on being totally independent of them, his teaching can be seen as a rarefied distillation of the highest ideals of the Hindu-Buddhist spiritual outlook which aims at final liberation.

***kriyā*** action, practice, ritual performance.

**Kriyā Yoga** ('active' yoga) the part of yoga practice which uses procedures requiring effort; a type of yoga which employs ritual as one of its techniques; a type of yoga which utilizes active involvement in life for spiritual progress, which may mean a variety of Karma Yoga or may also refer to the left-handed Tantric yoga approach. In the early times when yoga was the prerogative of *śramaṇas*, the renunciates, Kriyā Yoga was the hard preliminary stage requiring the adoption of the ascetic way of life, dedicated study of the scriptures or teachings of the chosen school or master, and total self-surrender to him or to the Lord or to the goal of liberation, in order to prepare oneself for the higher stage of meditative absorptions and discriminative vision leading to the realization of the goal. In the context of modern popularized yoga practice Kriyā Yoga means, besides the optional adoption of Hatha Yoga practice, incorporating into one's working life principles compatible with the goal, thereby enhancing the prospects of progress in one's regular meditative sessions.

**Kṛṣṇa** ('the black one') the eighth major incarnation of Viṣṇu. He is worshipped in two distinct forms. First, he apeared in the role of a playful pastoral god. He was born to Devakī, a cousin of Kaṁsa, the tyrant-king of Mathura who heard a prophecy that a son of hers would destroy him and therefore had her children put to death when they were born. When she conceived for the seventh time, it was with Balarāma, and as a part incarnation of Viṣṇu he was miraculously transferred from her womb into that of another wife of her husband. Kṛṣṇa was then born as her actual seventh child and, being a full incarnation of Viṣṇu, the birth was kept secret by his divine power. He was then taken by his father Vasudeva across the river Yamunā to the woods of Vṛndāvāna, where he was adopted by Yaśodā and Nada, a cowherding couple, who passed him off as their own son. When Kaṁsa discovered that Devakī did give birth to a son who was spirited away, he ordered the slaughter of all the male infants of his realm (cf. the Biblical story of the 'slaughter of the innocents'), but both sets of parents managed to escape with Balarāma, his mother and Kṛṣṇa to Gokula. Kṛṣṇa grew up playing many pranks, performing miraculous deeds and sporting with *gopīs* whom he charmed by playing his flute, making them fall madly in love with him. All this came to be interpreted as symbolizing the divine *līlā* and as an allegory of the mystical love between God and his devotees. In his other role, he appeared as the mature divine teacher who revealed the teachings of the BhG to Arjuna and showed himself to him as the Supreme Lord of the universe. While being revered as to date the most important incarnation of Viṣṇu in mainstream Hinduism, he has a large sectarian following as the Supreme Lord and is the centre of an extremely popular *bhakti* cult.

***kṛta*** made, finished, accomplished; the throw of dice of four.

**Kṛta Yuga** the first age of a *mahāyuga* in the Purāṇic world history (the Golden age of Gr. mythology), lasting 1,728,000 years; it is also called Satya Yuga, the age of truth.

***kṣatra*** power, domination, supremacy.

***kṣatriya*** warrior, prince, aristocrat; a member of the second of the four main Hindu castes (*varṇas*).

***kṣetra*** field; battlefield. Symbolically: body; the world.

***kṣetrajña*** ('the knower of the field') the inner self; the universal self or *ātman*.

**Kubera, Kuvera** god of wealth, ruler of the North and of lower deities such as *yakṣas* and *guhyakas*. He possessed a self-moving aerial car of palatial dimensions called Puṣpaka and his mount is a dwarf *yakṣa*.

***kula*** family, lineage; spiritual community.

***kuladevatā*** household or family deity.

***kumāra*** boy, prince; the appearance of Brahma who usually reveals himself to lower deities or to people in the form of a beautiful sixteen-year-old youth.

**Kumāra** another name of Kārttikeya or Skanda, the god of war. Kālidāsa described his birth in his poem *Kumārasaṁbhava.*

***kumārī*** virgin; princess; virtuous lady; goddess. The expression is often applied as a title, e.g. to Sītā, sometimes also to Durgā.

***kuṁbha*** pot, pitcher. A type of pitcher works as a symbol of motherhood, fertility and plenty, and is, or used to be, placed by villagers in the fields.

**Kuṁbha Mātā** the village goddess of fertility.

**Kuṁbha Mela** religious gathering of Hindu renunciates of all traditions held in twelve-year cycles, i.e. every three years in rotation, at Prayāga, Hardwār, Nāsik and Ujjain, the four places where according to legend fell some drops of *amṛta*, a drink of immortality, when gods and demons fought over it. The name is derived from the golden pitcher in which the drink of immortality was kept. The first historical evidence for this festival, which has always attracted enormous numbers of pilgrims, dates from the reign of the Emperor Harṣa.

***kuṇḍalinī*** ('the coiled one') man's spiritual potency, often referred to as *kuṇḍalinī śakti* or the 'serpent power'. It is supposedly coiled at the base of the spine (in the subtle body). When it is activated by the techniques of Kuṇḍalinī Yoga it rises along the spine through the central channel (*suṣumṇa nadī*) and awakens six spiritual centres (*cakras*) on the way, until it reaches the seventh centre called 'the thousand-petalled lotus' (*sahasrara padma*) at the top of the skull or above, which is the point of contiguity where the individual and the universal meet, whereupon enlightenment takes place.

***kūrma*** the cosmic turtle or tortoise, a symbol of the universe. Its lower shell represents the earth, the upper shell heavens and the body the interim world (cf. SB 6,1,1,12). Because of its capacity of withdrawing its limbs and head into its shell, it is also the symbol of the withdrawal of attention from the senses in the process of yogic concentration on the inner core.

**Kūrma** the second main incarnation of Viṣṇu which he undertook to facilitate the churning of the cosmic ocean by serving as a base for Mount Mandara so that it could easily be turned.

**Kurukṣetra** the battlefield on which the war between the Kauravas and Pāṇḍavas was fought and the BhG revealed. Metaphorically: the battlefield of righteousness, because issues of right and wrong were involved in the war and were being discussed in the BhG. Symbolically: the human body as the battlefield of the mind with the senses on which the battle for man's liberation is fought and won or lost. On this level of allegorical interpretation the setting and context in which the teachings on liberation and ways of achieving it are outlined by Kṛṣṇa to Arjuna appear in a new light, so far little commented on.

***kuśa*** a species of grass, *Desmostachya bipinnata*, regarded as most sacred. It was spread out on Vedic altars and the adjoining sacrificial area and burnt after the ritual. It is used by some ascetics for mats to sit on during meditation.

**Kuṣāna** the name for a conglomerate of tribal groups, most of them of IE stock, extant in Central Asia, East Iran and Afghanistan, who penetrated to India at the turn of our era. The bulk of them may have been Tocharians (known as Yüe-chi in Chinese), allied to Parthians (Pahlavas) mixed with contingents of Scythians (Śakas). The Kuṣāna dynasty established an empire in the first century A.D. stretching from North India to Central Asia, thereby opening the route for the spread of Hindu and Buddhist influences to Central Asia, China and the Far East. Kaniṣka I founded Puruṣapura (modern Peshawar) cca 120 A.D. and patronized Buddhism while fully respecting other religions.

**Kuvera** the earth spirit in AV (8,10,28); god of wealth (Kubera).

***lakh*** (Skt. *lakṣa*) a large number, usually 'a hundred thousand'.

***lakṣaṇa*** mark, sign; symbol.

**Lakṣmana** Rāma's half-brother who accompanied him and Sītā into banishment and helped him in her recovery when she was abducted, as narrated in the epic Rāmāyaṇa. He is regarded as a part incarnation of Viṣṇu or his snake Śeṣa.

**Lakṣmī** also known as Śrī Lakṣmī or simply Śrī. She emerged, with a lotus in her hand, from the froth of the cosmic ocean (cf. the birth of Aphrodite/Venus) in the course of its churning by gods and titans to obtain the drink of immortality. Viṣṇu took her for his wife and she underwent many incarnations alongside him, e.g. as Sītā with Rāma or Rukminī with Kṛṣṇa. Another tradition regards her as the primeval Goddess who appeared on the cosmic waters at the beginning of creation, floating on a lotus flower. In her own right she is the goddess of beauty, good luck and plenty and she is also said to have been the mother of Kāma, the god of love. As Viṣṇu's *śakti* she is the sustaining force in the universe and forms with him the dual deity called Lakṣmī-Nārāyaṇa, symbolizing the transcendental unity of opposites in the absolute *brahman* or *paramātman*.

**Lakulīśa** the legendary founder of Pāśupatas who lived in the early second century A.D., the author of *Pāśupatasūtra*. He is regarded by some followers as an incarnation of Śiva and is represented as a naked ithyphallic yogi (with a staff, *lakuṭa*, in his left hand, hence his name) and sometimes with animals, including a pair of deer. He is reminiscent, through some of these features, of the Harappan icon of the so-called proto-Śiva.

***lalita*** m.: the name of a musical scale; n.: sport, play, charm, elegance; a dance form in Śiva's cosmic dance.

***lalitā*** a poetic metre; a musical mode; woman; seductive woman.

**Lalitā** a name of Pārvatī when dancing (and representing thereby the hidden dynamic source about to give birth to manifestation); the name of one of the ten Mahāvidyās or Tantric multiple forms of the Goddess used in ritual *maṇḍalas* of female deities, often as the central presiding one.

**Laṅkā** the name of the island and its capital described in the Rāmāyaṇa as the seat of the demon king Rāvaṇa who abducted Sītā. Originally the summit of Mount Meru, it was broken off by Vāyu, the god of wind, and thrown into the sea, thus becoming an island.

**Law** in Hinduism: the recognition of the feature of regularity and reliability built into the fabric of reality and understood as a force which is inherent to existence on all levels: material, mental, moral and spiritual. It was known as *ṛta* in the Vedas and when applied to human values, it became *dharma*. In the ethical sphere it makes its impact as the karmic process securing the reaping of the fruits of the deeds of individuals in their present life or in future lives. On the social level the law is a reflection of the higher cosmic order. Because of human ignorance and ability to make unwise choices which are not in harmony with the cosmic order, laws which should reflect it have to be formulated by law-givers for the guidance of people and need enforcement by authority if disregarded. This should ideally be backed by a higher sanction, i.e. by the achievement of sagehood as in the case of the legendary ancient law-givers, and in the case of kings by the possession of a true inner link to the transcendent source of royal power which makes a king into a *dharmarāja* and justifies his right to *daṇḍa*, i.e. to the enforcement of authority by punishing the wrong-doer. In practice the recorded historical law-givers based their human laws on the notion of *ṛta* backed by the exegesis from scriptures (*śruti*), which led to the creation of a kind of sacred tradition (*smṛti*), and the king obtained his divine link by ritual consecration which gave him the divine sanction in the eyes of his subjects, but did not necessarily guarantee his righteous conduct and rule.

***laya*** dissolution (of the world at the end of the world period called *kalpa*, i.e. the end of a Brahma's day); meditative absorption.

**Laya Yoga** a Tantric meditation technique in which the personality dissolves and merges with the deity or enters its original state outside creation.

**Levirate** (*niyoga*) the marriage of a widow to a brother-in-law, or in some cases to another close in-law relative, mainly to produce offspring on behalf of the deceased one. It was practised in ancient times and continued on a minor scale, where *satī* was not enforced, till the last century when it was endorsed even by Dayānanda, but rejected by other reform movements.

**Liberation** (*mokṣa*) refers in Hinduism to the final state of salvation and is invariably understood as a state of freedom from the necessity of being born in temporary and limited forms of existence, although it does not exclude the possibility of birth of the liberated one in saṁsāric realms by choice and for a purpose.

***līlā*** play, game; divine play or game, a concept resorted to by Bādarāyaṇa and other Vedāntic authors to 'explain' the 'reason' or motive for the creation of the world by the omnipotent, omniscient, eternal and self-sufficient Supreme Lord. This notion is also symbolized by the legendary games and pranks of Kṛṣṇa. Śiva's cosmic dance is also sometimes referred to as *līlā* and it then symbolizes the global repetitive game of manifestation in its three phases of *sṛṣṭi* (emerging), *sthiti* (duration) and *saṁhara* (withdrawal).

***liṅga*** mark, sign, token; emblem, symbol, characteristic; gender; male organ of generation (*śiśna*); image of god, particularly of Śiva, in the shape of the male organ, expressing his creative power. It is often just a plain column rounded at the top, thus becoming an uniconic representation of the transcendent or of the absolute reality and its creative power, referred to as *liṅga svayambhū* (self-existent *liṅga*). In this form it also symbolizes the cosmic pillar, Mount Meru and the *axis mundi* which penetrates all levels of reality. When rounded also at the bottom so that it becomes egg-shaped, it stands for Hiraṇyagarbha. A frequent form of the *liṅga* as a centre of worship in temples dedicated to Śiva is a rounded pillar set in a circular stone, representing the *yoni*, which has a groove with a spout for draining *ghee* and liquids from ceremonial washing. As a twin symbol the *liṅga-yoni* effigy represents the polarity of phenomenal reality, but by its union it points to the transcendental unity of godhead.

***liṅga śarīra*** ('body of characteristics') the name for the causal body, also known as *kāraṇa śarīra*, which bears the marks of the individual's *karma* and is its carrier during his transmigration from life to life.

**Liṅgāyata** a Śaiva movement in Southern India, also known as Vīraśaiva, founded by Basava in the twelfth century, which superseded the declining Kālamukha sect. It recognized the equality of women and abolished caste distinctions and the authority of brahmins. Five new lines of priesthood were introduced instead, derived from the five faces of Śiva manifested on his *pañcamukhaliṅga* (five-faced *liṅga*). The teaching is a kind of Advaitism: Śiva is the sole reality called *śiva-tattva* in the unmanifest state. By the activation of his *śakti* he manifests as *liṅga-sthala* or Śiva the Lord and as *aṅga-sthala* in multiple form as all individual beings, his worshippers. This means that the individual is identical with him, but this fact is obscured by *māyā*. The goal of unification is realized by the individual in meditation by contemplating the personal *śivaliṅga* enclosed in a small ball, worn as a pendant round the neck. It is symbolical of the identity of the individual with the universe and with Śiva in his *tattva* state. The sect uses, during congregational sessions, so-called *vacanas* (pronouncements), i.e. short lyrical exhortations. Poems and devotional songs are also frequent in communal worship. Some of these were composed by Basava himself, but over 200 authors are counted among their composers.

***loka*** place, world, world division; sphere or plane of existence. Different schools describe different world divisions. Broadly speaking three worlds (*triloka*) are envisaged: infernal, terrestrial and heavenly. The popular Purāṇic division of the world lists, besides hells, seven regions: (1) Bhur (terrestrial sphere); (2) Bhuvar (intermediary realm, the domicile of *munis* and *siddhas*, popularly placed between the earth and heaven); (3) Svar (Indra's heaven, in popular view between the sun and the polar star); (4) Maharloka (the domicile of saintly clans); (5) Janloka (the abode of the sons of Brahma); (6) Taparloka (the seat of accomplished ascetics); (7) Satyaloka (the plane of truth, also called Brahmaloka).

**Lokapāla(s)** guardians of the world, presiding over directions (each assisted by an elephant): Indra - E; Agni - SE; Yama - S; Sūrya - SW; Varuṇa - W; Vāya - NW; Kuvera - N; Soma - NE. (There are variations.)

**Lokāyata** a name for the teachings of Carvāka which regards only this material world as real.

**Lokeśvara** 'the Lord of the Universe', one of the many Mahāyāna cosmic Buddhas (known from the Buddhist text Sukhāvatī Vyūha as Lokeśvararāja, the Buddha of a previous world period). He became popular in areas where Buddhism and Hinduism mixed such as Nepal and South East Asia and is described sometimes as Buddha and sometimes as a Bodhisattva or as God. He is often depicted with four heads, as is god Brahma, and he is also associated with the cult of Śiva who is supposed to have merged with him.

**Mā** (mother) short for Mother Goddess.

***mada*** intoxication; intoxicating drink, one of the ingredients of the left-handed Tantric ritual of the five M's.

**Madhva** (twelfth-thirteenth century A.D.) a South Indian brahmin, wandering Vaiṣṇava preacher and the author of a compendium of philosophical systems called *Sarvadarśaṇasaṅgraha*. A committed opponent of Advaita Vedānta, he founded the Dvaita or dualistic school of Vedānta which teaches plurality of selves or personalities as continuing in existence even in the state of liberation, although remaining dependent on God. It has been suggested that in his teaching on the possibility of eternal damnation and some other features of his theology he was influenced by Christianity which he may have known from contacts with Syrian Christians in Malabar.

**Magadha** a kingdom in North East India in the Buddha's time which subsequently expanded to cover the area of modern Bihār and West Bengal. It became the nucleus of the Mauryan Empire with its capital Pātaliputra (Patna). In the early Vedic time it was the territory of the non-Vedic but Āryan Vrātya fraternities living outside the domain of the Vedic civilization, but it was later included and brahmanized, with parts of Vrātya spiritual lore codified in the AV. A number of non-Vedic spiritual movements seem to have originated there, among them Buddhism and Jainism.

**Magic** a set of tenets and practices concerned with achieving desired results by controlling the occult forces of the universe (cosmic intelligences, spirits) through ritual and mental means. It is not part of Hinduism as a religion and spiritual path, but an element of magic is present in the sacrificial ritual when it is aimed at specific results, and in the traditional belief of orthodox Pūrva Mīmāṁsā followers in the absolute certainty of the outcome of correctly performed rituals. Magic powers (*siddhis*) are moreover believed to accompany spiritual progress in yoga or on the path to liberation, but their use other than in helping others on the path and in spreading the liberating teaching is equivalent to going astray and precludes attainment of the goal of liberation.

**Mahābalipuram** see Māmallapuram.

***mahābhāgavata*** the 'great devotee' of the Lord Kṛṣṇa, applied usually to those who worship him as the Supreme Lord.

**Mahābhārata** the 'great epic of the Bharatas', the longest epic poem in the world, of great importance to Hindus, which describes the events before, during and after the ferocious war between the Kauravas and Pāṇḍavas, and deals on many occasions with questions of morality and duty and with many religious topics, including the meaning of life, salvation and the ways of achieving it. The Purāṇic tradition has it that the great war took place in 3102 B.C. and that with it started the present dark age of human history (Kali Yuga), but if there is a historical reality behind it, it will have taken place after 1000 B.C. Begun in the mist of those early times, the epic started taking its familiar shape from around the third century B.C. and grew over subsequent centuries by constant elaboration and additions of further episodes for perhaps another 600 more years, although some interpolations occurred later still. Tradition attributes the authorship of the epic to Kṛṣṇa Dvaipāyana, a legendary figure known as Vyāsa (the arranger), who himself appears in the epic, participating in the events.

***mahābhūtas*** 'great elements', the four substances or elemental forces which constitute the material world: *pṛthivī* (earth, solidity), *āpas* (water, fluidity), *vāyu* (air, vibration) and *agni* (fire, warmth, light), with *ākāśa* (ether, space) added as a fifth one in some systems. In monistic teachings such as Advaita Vedānta they are the last or grossest emanations of the one divine source; in other systems such as Sāṅkhya they are the products of the forces of nature (*prakṛti*).

**Mahādeva** ('great god') an appellation of Śiva frequently used by his devotees, especially when thinking of him as the transcendent Absolute. His consort Pārvatī is then called Mahādevī and is referred to in this context as his *śakti*. In the original state of unity of the two, they stand for the unmanifest (*avyakta*) reality. When they assume separate forms, they then enter into an active union which gives rise to the manifestation of the world (*sṛṣṭi*) represented by the twin Trimūrti, i.e. the three gods Brahma, Viṣṇu and Śiva with spouses as their *śaktis*. In her own right Mahādevī is one of the names of the highest goddess of the Śākta cults.

**Mahākāla** ('great time') the name of Śiva as destroyer.

**Mahānavamī** the great nine day festival of the Goddess, usually under the name of Durgā; see Durgāpūjā.

***mahāpralaya*** 'the great dissolution' of the universe at the end of a Brahma's life when the whole of manifested reality with all its beings is re-absorbed into the transcendental divine source (variously named according to the school of thought or sect: Vṛtra, *aja*, *brahman*, Śiva, Viṣṇu Jalaśāyin etc.) for a period of rest. This is followed by a new creation which starts with the birth of a new Brahma and the rebirth of unliberated beings from the previous world period.

***mahārātrī*** the 'great night', the period of rest between the end of one great world period and the start of the next manifestation of the universe (or between the death of one Brahma and the birth of the next).

**Maharloka** see *loka*.

***mahārṣi*** (Maharishi) great seer; used originally for only a few seers of the Vedas by tradition regarded as on a level with gods, it later became, and is still today, a much used and sometimes misused honorific title of spiritual teachers or *gurus*. It is also used for the legendary seven *ṛṣis* who had a great reputation for wisdom, although no specific teachings of theirs are known and the lists of their names differ.

***mahāsukha*** 'great happiness', a term used by left-hand Tantric systems for the experience of *samādhi* in the *maithuna* context.

**Mahat** (the equivalent of Buddhi) the Cosmic Mind or Universal Intelligence, the first evolute of the Absolute in the process of world manifestation. The term is used in some systems which avoid theistic terminology.

**Mahātma** an honorific title of great and respected personalities.

***mahātman*** the great (universal) self.

***mahāvākya*** great pronouncement; 'great dictum'; 'Great Saying'. Usually four great Upaniṣadic sayings or utterances are meant, all of them asserting the basic identity of the universal and the individual, of the essence of reality as a whole and the innermost self of man (*brahman*=*ātman*) which is the foundation of all Vedāntic monistic systems, although the interpretations of this equation differ in details according to the school. The sayings are: *aham brahmāsmi* (I am *brahman*, BU 1,4,10); *tat tvam asi* ('thou art that', CU 6,8,7; 6,9,4; 6,14,3); *ayam ātmā brahma* (this self is *brahman*, BU 4,4,5); and *sarvaṅ khalvidam brahma* (all this is verily *brahman*, CU 3,14,1). Others are sometimes added, the most significant among them being: *prajñānam brahma* (*brahman* is wisdom [or intelligence], AU 3,3,).

**Mahāvidyā** the Tantric goddess of transcendental wisdom, sometimes identified with Aditi; in pl. Mahāvidyās represent the forces of *māyā* or the universal creative powers, emanating from the Goddess, and her capacity to produce the concrete complicated web of manifested life, both in its positive (productive) and its negative (catastrophic or destructive) aspects. They are depicted as goddesses, each representing a particular aspect of manifested reality, e.g. Lalitā (space) or Tāra (time).

**Mahāvīra** 'great hero', a title designating a person of the highest spiritual achievement, mostly applied to Vardhamāna (cca 599–467 B.C.), the historical founder of Jainism. He was of the Nāta (Skt. Jñātri) clan from Vaiśālī, the capital of Videha (now in Bihār). Before going his own way after his renunciation, he was associated with Gośāla, the founder of the Ājīvikas. The Jain tradition maintains that after a life of teaching and leading his community of ascetic followers he starved himself to death at the age of 72 at Pāra near Rājagṛha (today's Rajgir).

***mahāvrata*** the 'great vow'; applied in the context of different schools to initial vows or preliminary disciplines required for successful practice of the spiritual path and progress on it, e.g. *yama* or moral restrictions on Patañjali's yoga path.

**Mahāvrāta** an ancient village festival connected originally with the winter solstice as the beginning of the new year cycle. However, it gradually shifted towards the spring to become the beginning of the agricultural year and was celebrated with fertility rites which included games, races, dances, erotic scenes and ritual coition. Some elements of this festival survive under different labels such as the Holī festival.

**Mahāyāna** the 'great vehicle' school of Buddhism notable for its Bodhisattva doctrine and the system of Cosmic Buddhas.

***mahāyuga*** a period of Purāṇic world history, lasting 4,320,000 years, divided into four *yugas* or ages: Kṛta, Tretā, Dvāpara and Kali Yuga.

**Maheśvara** Great Lord; a name of Śiva used by his followers, who regard him as the Supreme Lord. Maheśvarī: the Goddess when she functions as his *śakti*.

***mahiṣa*** buffalo; the emblem of Yama (and of Jain *tīrthaṅkaras*).

**Mahiṣa, Mahiṣāsura** the buffalo-demon, a one-time usurper of the position of gods and their oppressor. They created (or evoked) the goddess Durgā to rid themselves of him and she killed him, thereby acquiring the name Mahiṣāsuramardiṇi.

***maithuna*** sexual union, marriage; spiritual marriage; one of the rites in the left-handed Tantric ritual of the five M's.

**Maitreya** (Pl. Metteya) the name of the future Buddha.

***makara*** a mythical crocodile-like sea animal, adopted by Varuṇa as his mount. He is also the emblem of Kāma, the god of love, and is believed to enhance fertility.

***makāra*** the performance of the Tantric ritual of the five M's.

***mālā*** garland; a string of beads ('rosary') used during recitation or inner repetition of *mantras* as an aid in counting.

**Māmallapuram** (Mahābalipuram) a complex of smaller-sized temples and shrines carved out of rocks on the coast south of Madrās built under the Pallava dynasty and dated cca seventh century A.D. The site also has a large bas-relief on a rock face representing the descent of Gaṅgā from heaven (sometimes wrongly named 'Arguna's Penance').

***maṁsa*** meat; one of the ingredients in the left-handed Tantric ritual of the five M's.

***manas*** mind; intellect; psyche; spirit.

**Mānasa** a sacred lake in the Himālayas, the mythical terrestrial, though not actual, source of Gaṅgā.

**Mānava Dharma Śāstra** Manu's Code of Law.

**Mandākinī** the name of the celestial Gaṅgā before her descent to earth, in popular perception identified with the Milky Way.

***maṇḍala*** circle; a circular diagram which can be simple or very elaborate and is used for rituals and meditation. The complex ones symbolize the universe with all its hierarchical regions as well as the human personality and its inner layers. Even some Hindu temples are designed or can be viewed as grand *maṇḍalas*, but it was the Buddhist tradition which developed its stūpas into impressive macro/microcosmic statements such as Bodhnath in Nepal or Borobudur on Java. The latter is also a symbolical depiction of and instruction about the way to enlightenment.

***maṇḍala-nṛtya*** a circular dance; Kṛṣṇa performed it as the sole partner of his *gopīs*, whirling from one to the other so quickly that none of them noticed his absences from her. This symbolizes the infinite potential of God for a full mystic union in *bhakti* with each and every one of his devotees.

***maṇḍapa*** canopy; tent; pavilion; ceremonial hall; pillared hall; the main hall of a Hindu temple, originally covered with a flat roof, later often with a dome over it, and raised on a moulded plinth.

**Mandara** the mountain used by the gods and titans for churning the cosmic ocean to obtain the drink of immortality. It was supported for the purpose by the turtle incarnation of Viṣṇu.

***mandāra*** coral tree, *Erythrina indica*.

**Mandāra** the coral tree in Indra's paradise which enables its inhabitants to remember their past lives when they smell its fragrance.

***mandir*(*a*)** dwelling; mansion; dwelling-place of god; temple; also used to denote the subsidiary halls in Hindu temple complexes.

**Mandodaka** the name of a mythical lake in the transcendent region of Mount Kailāsa said to be the source of the heavenly Gaṅgā.

***mangala*** blessing; *maṇgalācaraṇa* – a salutation address, usually in verses, opening a written work and usually directed to a deity.

***mani*** pearl; ornament; jewel; magic jewel; cf. *cintamani.*

***maṇipūra*** (gem-filled) ***cakra*** the centre of energy in the subtle body opposite the navel in the shape of a ten-petalled lotus.

***manomaya kośa*** ('mind-made sheath') a Vedāntic term for the 'mental' body in the system of five sheaths, the other four *kośas* being: *annamaya*, *prāṇamaya, vijñānamaya* and *ānandamaya*

***mantra*** verbal means of communicating with and influencing the transcendent which in ancient times were, for most purposes, Vedic verses. They were recited as *mantras* during rituals by the appropriate priests: RV by *hotar*, SV by *udgātar*, YV by *adhvaryu* and AV by the supervising brahmin. On some occasions short pronouncements were uttered before or after the recitation of the verses, some of which did not have an obvious meaning, but symbolical or magical significance was ascribed to them. A *mantra* can now be defined as a verbal expression which may be a syllable, a word or a whole phrase used for recitation, chanting, or verbal meditation, aloud or internally in the course of worship. The use of *mantras* for spiritual purposes (the *japa* meditational method) is sometimes referred to as Mantra Yoga and was promoted particularly by Tantrism, which is therefore referred to also as Mantrayāna. In recent times a type of Mantra Yoga has been popularized in the West by Mahesh Yogi's movement as TM ('transcendental meditation').

**Manu** the patriarch of mankind; the first man and patriarch of mankind in each subperiod of Purāṇic world history called

Manvantara who, according to medieval Purāṇic tradition, obtained his wife from his rib (a probable influence of the Bible). Manu is also the name of the supposed author of the first known systematic treatment of Hindu law variously named as Manu Smṛti, Manu Saṁhitā or Mānavadharmaśāstra, dated between 600 B.C. and A.D. 300, which is probably a work of several generations. It contains the code of law, customs based on the Vedic tradition, customs established by precedents, and even an outline of the ultimate goal as salvation through union with *brahman*.

**Manvantara** a period in Purāṇic world history which starts with a renewal after a previous collapse of civilization. According to one theory it equals a *mahāyuga* (4,320,000 years), but another theory divides the *kalpa* into fourteen Manvantaras, which would extend the duration of each Manvantara over more than seventy-one *mahāyugas*, so that it would then amount to 308,571,428 years. Each Manvantara is presided over by a new Manu.

**Manyu** the Vedic god of anger or wrath.

**Māra** (death) an epithet of Kāma. It is a seldom mentioned aspect of the god of love. Since he presides over sensual love, which is possible only in the saṁsāric realm of birth and death, he is virtually luring beings to repeated death by ensnaring them in bonds of love.

***mārga*** way, path; religious path to salvation.

**Marriage** (*vivāha*) is a major sacrament (*saṁskāra*) in Hinduism which lasts, according to Manu, for all successive lives, and therefore widows should not remarry. The main duty in marriage is to produce offspring and erotic satisfaction. The consummation of a marriage (*samāpana*) should be approached gently and gradually and should occur on the fourth or tenth night. The usual age for marriage at the time of the Guptas was thirteen to sixteen years, but already in Vedic times the tendency to marry girls before they reached puberty had made itself felt sporadically. Gradually the age was lowered and child marriage came to be accepted, particularly after the Islamic conquest, until reform movements started opposing it. Levirate (*niyoga*) was practised in Vedic and epic times and sporadically later as well. Remarriage did, however, occur in some quarters and has been advocated by reformers since the last century. The modern Marriage Act, permitting also divorce, was passed in the Indian republic in 1955. Marriage rites vary greatly according to caste and Vedic marriage rituals are still in use, albeit in a shortened form.

**Mārtāṇḍa** an Āditya, i.e. a son of Aditi. He is a form of the Sun god. Aditi gave birth to him and then cast him away to die only to bring him back again (RV 10,72,8–9), which is a mythological idea, expressing the metaphorical image that the sun is born every morning and dies in the evening.

**Maruts** a troop (*gaṇa*) of Vedic storm deities in the retinue of Rudra and therefore called also Rudras or Rudriyas. They manifest in lightning, ride on the wind and assist in bringing rain.

***māsa*** moon; lunar month; a measure of time based on the lunar division of the year into 27 *nakṣatras*, i.e. lunar phases between full moon and new moon.

***māta, mātar, mātṛ, mā*** mother; mother's womb; mother Earth.

**Matariśvan** a Vedic god associated with domestic fire, the bringer of fire from heaven to human homes. The name is explained as coming from the process of kindling fire by friction. A flat piece of wood, called *mātar*, 'mother', with a small depression in it, was used as a base, and a pointed firestick (*araṇi*) was placed in the depression and quickly turned using a bow-string. Thus kindled, Mātariśvan is nevertheless understood as akin to the lightning, the fire from heaven, and to god Agni. (There seem to be traces here of an IE myth which led also to the Gr. Promethean myth.)

***maṭh(a)***, (vern. *mutt*) an ascetic or monastic community; a monastic establishment; a monastic teaching institution of the Śaṅkarite Advaita Vedānta.

**Mathurā** (vern. Mattra, Muttra) a city on the banks of the river Yamunā with a strong Buddhist past, later overlaid by the Kṛṣṇa legend, and celebrated as his birthplace. It is one of the seven sacred Hindu cities.

***mātṛkās*** 'little mothers', mystical syllables in *cakras* and other diagrams, emanating power and regarded as female deities (*śaktis*) who also symbolize fecundity; see also *saptamātṛkās*.

***matsya*** fish; one of the ingredients in the left-handed Tantric ritual of the five M's.

**Matsya** the first major incarnation of Viṣṇu as a fish which advised Manu to build a ship to save himself from the deluge and to provide for the preservation of seeds and animals.

**Matsyendranāth** (ninth to tenth century) the legendary first incarnate teacher of the Nātha Yogi movement and the reputed founder of the Hatha Yoga system (together with his pupil Gorakhnāth).

***mauna*** sagehood; the vow of silence.

**Maurya** the first imperial dynasty of India (cca 321–180 B.C.), founded by Chandragupta (cca 321–297 B.C.) whose grandson was the great and celebrated ruler Aśoka.

***māyā*** illusion; magic; phenomenal reality; the illusory nature of phenomenal reality; the creative power of God, often represented by his female consort and virtually identical with his *śakti*.

**Māyā** a name of the Goddess, especially under her aspect as Durgā, called also Māyādevī and Mahāmāyā.

**Meditation** is an important part of the Hindu religious approach. It ranges from pious verbal contemplation of a text to silent concentration and total spiritual absorption brought about by advanced yoga techniques.

**Meru** (also: Sumeru) in Purāṇic legends it is the mythical golden mountain which represents the axis of the world, along which are centred all spheres of existence, from the highest heaven at the summit down to its foot where there are the eight cities of the Lokapālas. Then comes man's world and beneath it seven nether worlds. The mountain is supported on the sevenfold hood of the coiled snake Vāsuki, who causes an earthquake each time he yawns. At the end of the great world period he uncoils and the world is consumed in his fiery breath.

**Mīmāṁsā** see Purva Mīmāṁsā.

**Mīnākṣī** ('fish-eyed') a South Indian goddess, a daughter of Kubera and a wife of Śiva, regarded by some as an incarnation of Pārvatī and installed in one of the greatest South Indian temples in Madura.

**Mīrabaī** (fifteenth to sixteenth century) a legendary Rājput princess turned poetess and mystic whose *bhajans* to Kṛṣṇa are still popular. Married to the Rāṇa of Udaipur, she eventually escaped home life and wandered off to Vṛndāvan in pursuit of her spiritual vocation.

***mithuna*** couple, pair; depiction of an 'amatory couple' in relief, usually on doors of houses and temples, regarded as auspicious and pointing to creation symbology; cf. *maithuna*.

**Mitra** in the Vedic Pantheon he is one of the Ādityas and a close associate of Varuṇa. He oversees community affairs and is the guardian of laws, contracts, bonds of friendship and love. Known to Iranians as Mithra, he became the chief deity of Mithraism, a religion of Hellenistic and Roman times, temporarily a rival of Christianity.

***mleccha*** foreigner; barbarian; member of a non-Āryan race, not necessarily regarded as inferior to Āryans, e.g. Greeks (Yavanas) in ancient times or the British in colonial times.

***modaka*** rice cake, sweetmeat ball (favoured by Gaṇeśa).

***moha*** delusion; a flaw in human perception leading one to mistake products of *māyā* for true reality.

**Mohinī** Viṣṇu's female form. He assumed the shape of a beautiful woman to charm *asuras* and cheat them out of their share of *amṛta* after the churning of the cosmic ocean. On another occasion he took the form to seduce Śiva when he was engaged in asceticism.

***mokṣa*** liberation; the final release from the round of rebirths.

**Mokṣa Dharma** a text inserted into the bulk of the Mhb and dealing with philosophical questions of life and liberation, with many overlaps with pre-classical Sāṅkhya thought.

***mudrā*** sign, symbol; gesture; ritual gesture; symbolical gesture; dance position; womb. In the Tantric ritual of the five M's it may mean: (1) the female partner; (2) parched grain and kidneys (regarded as aphrodisiac); (3) a particular symbolical gesture peculiar to the ritual of the five M's. There is some obscurity as to which of these three meanings represents the actual fourth 'M' in the ritual. It may vary from sect to sect.

***mukhaliṅga*** a conically shaped column with one or more faces carved in relief on it, usually representing various aspects of Śiva.

***mukti*** the same as *mokṣa*.

***mūlādhāra*** (root-holding) ***cakra*** the spiritual centre located at the base of the spine in the subtle body. It is in the shape of a four-petalled lotus, as taught by Kuṇḍalinī Yoga.

***muni*** sage; in the RV it means a sage of a non-traditional type, such as the 'long-haired one' (*keśin*); later the word was applied to the Buddha (Śakyamuni); in the context of Hindu religious practices it is used to denote silent sages, hence *mauna*.

***muñja*** a kind of rush; tall, sedge-like grass, regarded as ritually pure and used for making the brahmins' sacred cords.

***mūrti*** shape, form; body, figure; image, representation of a deity (sometimes still inappropriately translated as 'idol').

**Murugan** (Murukaṉ=Kumāra) the Tamil name of the god of war (i.e. Skanda or Kārttikeya).

***mūṣa, mūṣka*** mouse, rat; Gaṇeśa's mount and guardian of his bowl of sweetmeat balls.

***nābha, nābhi*** navel, centre; the Vedic altar, the sacrificial altar (as the meeting-place of gods and men); the centre of the world or the central power point of universal energy (see RV 10,82,5; cf. the Gr. *omphalos* in Delphi). It is not the centre of the physical world, but rather the transcendental centre of the multi-dimensional world-complex, and by the same token the gate of creation (cf. the Vedic womb of Aditi) and the hidden central point of contiguity between the transcendent and phenomenal worlds. Also: a focus for meditation ('belly watching', an ancient method made known in modern times mainly as the Burmese Buddhist *vipassanā* meditation, but practised also in medieval Bulgarian monastic communities of Bogomils). In mythology: Viṣṇu's navel (with a lotus growing out of it while he is lying on the snake Ananta and Brahma is sitting on the lotus about to start the process of creation).

***nāḍī*** pipe; vein; also used for channels conducting *prāṇa* through the subtle body (*sukṣma śarīra*) according to the system of Kuṇḍalinī Yoga.

***nāga*** snake; a serpent-being; a category of lower deities dwelling on the bottom of seas and rivers or in their own underworld called Nāgaloka, one of the Pātālas. They appear as snakes, but can also take human form, sometimes befriending humans, and their females may take the shape of beautiful women and marry humans.

**Nāga tribes** Negroid tribal communities in East Assam.

***nāgarī*** 'town' script; see *devanāgarī*.

**Nāgās** (vern. from Skt. *nagna*, naked) a sect of naked ascetics from non-brahmin castes who are prepared to fight to defend the tradition. During the time of Muslim persecution they were affiliated to the Daśanāmī Order to defend its brahmin members who were not allowed to use force for their own protection. They have also been known to fight rival sects.

**Nāgī** the snake goddess worshipped mainly in South India as a form of Durgā.

***nakṣatra*** constellation; lunar mansion; the division of the moon's orbit among the stars into twenty-seven (sometimes twenty-eight) sections, regarded also as goddesses, the wives of the Moon god.

***nāma*** name; mentality; character.

***nāmakīrtana*** worship of one's chosen deity (*iṣṭa devatā*) by constant repetition (*japa*) of its name.

***nāmarūpa*** (name and form) the psychophysical compound forming the complete human person.

***namaskār, namaskāra mudrā*** salutation; a gesture of reverence made with palms touching and raised to one's forehead.

**Nānak** (1469–1538/9) the founder of Sikhism, referred to by his followers as Guru Nānak. He was born of a *kṣatriya* family and by profession was an accountant. After a religious experience he left his family and became a wanderer for some years before settling in Kartarpur, Pañjāb. Influenced by Sūfism and Kabīr, he preached religious toleration and praised one God in his *bhajans*. He accepted some of the Hindu doctrines such as transmigration, karmic retribution and the idea of salvation, but rejected the authority of the Vedas and the priesthood and the worship of Hindu gods as well as the caste system which, however, later crept back into Sikh communities in a partly modified form.

**Nandi** ('joyful') the name of Śiva's white bull, the chief of his attendants, his mount and emblem. As a primal image of strength, potency and the power of natural instincts, he becomes a symbol of moral and religious duty, justice and law, i.e. of *dharma*, when tamed or mastered (hence the image of 'riding the bull').

**Nandinī** the name of the cow of plenty, the wishing-cow, produced during the churning of the cosmic ocean.

***naraka*** hell as a place of torture and a temporary abode for evildoers who are reborn there to atone for their guilt before being born again in a human or some other world. Up to twenty-one subdivisions of hell are enumerated by various sources.

**Narasiṁha** man-lion, the fourth main incarnation of Viṣṇu, undertaken by him to slay the tyrant demon-king Hiraṇyakaśipu, who could not be killed by a man or an animal.

**Nārāyaṇa** ('moving on waters') originally the name for Prajāpati, Puruṣa or Brahma, i.e. for the demiurge god-creator (cf. the image of the spirit of God hovering above the waters in Genesis). Later it became one of the names of Viṣṇu, particularly in his *yoganidrā* state between two manifestations when he is reclining on the cosmic snake Ananta/Śeṣa and floating on the cosmic waters (symbolizing the latent creative forces at rest) between two world manifestations (in the state of *pralāya*). Some Purāṇic texts equate him with the Upaniṣadic *ātman*.

**Narmadā** (vern. Nerbudda) after Gaṅgā perhaps the most sacred Indian river. It is cherished for its pebbles which are naturally shaped so that they resemble the abstract, aniconic form of Śiva known as *liṅga svayambhū*, representing the unknowable Absolute which can be experienced only in liberation.

**Nāsatyas** see Aśvins.

**Nāsik** a sacred city in North India. According to legend some drops of *amṛta*, a drink of immortality, fell there and in three other places when gods and demons were fighting over it. This is commemorated by a Kuṁbha Mela every twelve years. The other places are: Hardwār (Haridvāra), Prayāga and Ujjain (Avanti).

***nāstika*** denying the authority of the Vedas, unorthodox. As noun the term is used not only for materialists and sceptics, but also for followers of non-orthodox religious movements such as Buddhism and Jainism.

**Naṭarāja** Śiva as the 'Lord of the Dance', symbolizing the cosmic process of repeated successive manifestations of the world, its periods of flowering and its periodic destruction.

***nātha*** lord; used mainly in compounds with names and titles, e.g. Jagannātha, the Lord of the World.

**Nātha cult** a Tantric sect of mixed origin with Taoist, Buddhist and Siddha cult connections which eventually crystallized into a Śaivite cult with esoteric yogic teachings and practices. These centre around the notion of the nectar of immortality issuing from the *sahasrara padma* and absorbed internally in order to transform the body into a vessel of immortality. Its first teacher is believed to have been Śiva as Ādinātha and its first human transmitter Matsyendranātha, the legendary teacher of Gorakhnātha.

***navagrahas*** the 'nine planets' of Indian astronomy and astrology. They are: Sūrya (sun), Soma or Candra (moon), Budha (Mercury), Śukra (Venus); Maṅgala or Aṅgāraka (Mars), Bṛhaspati (Jupiter), Śani (Saturn), Rāhu (the north or ascending lunar node) and Ketu (the south or descending node). The sun, moon and planets are regarded also as gods, while Rāhu and Ketu are demons, or perhaps one twin-demon, responsible for eclipses of the sun and moon while attempting to swallow them.

**Nāyaṉmārs** leading figures and poets of the South Indian Śaiva Siddhānta system.

**Neo-Hinduism** a term used sometimes in connection with Hindu reform movements marked by external influences, particularly from the European liberal tradition, but also from Islam, Christianity and nineteenth century evolutionary philosophy and universalism. Traces of neo-Hindu attitudes can also be found in the work of recent Hindu thinkers, e.g. in Radhakrishnan's early conception of Hinduism as a universal religion of the future and in Aurobindo's vision of the spiritualization of the whole world.

***neti neti*** 'not so, not so' (BU 4,2,4,) is an often quoted extract from Yājñavalkya's statement about the impossibility of giving an accurate and positive characterization of *ātman*, who is beyond conceptual grasp and can be known only by direct experience.

***nidrā*** sleep.

**Nidrā** the goddess of sleep, born out of the churning of the cosmic ocean, who unites with Viṣṇu for the period of *pralaya* when he rests on the waters, reclining on his snake.

**Nīlakaṇṭha** ('blue throat') an epithet of Śiva whose throat changed colour when he drank the poison produced from the churning of the cosmic ocean, to save living beings from death.

**Niṁbārka** a philosopher and teacher, possibly a contemporary of Madhva, influenced by him and also by Rāmānuja. He taught the Bhedābheda or Dvaitādvaita doctrine, a kind of compromise between dualism and non-dualism, according to which individuals and the world are both identical and different from God, although fully dependent on him. In his personal allegiance he was the follower of Kṛṣṇa whom he identified with *brahman*.

***nirguṇa*** 'without qualities', a designation for *brahman* by itself, i.e. the unmanifest absolute reality (cf. *saguṇa*).

**Nirṛti** goddess of decay and death, wife or daughter of Adharma.

***nirvāṇa*** the ultimate state of liberation from the round of rebirths (*saṁsāra*), used mainly in Buddhist and also Jain context, but later employed also in Hindu texts.

***nirvikalpa samādhi*** a term used in Jñāna Yoga for the deep state of meditational absorption beyond the subject-object duality. It is regarded as the threshold to the final realization.

***nivṛtti*** return, suspension; reabsorption of manifestation into its unmanifest source; abstaining from, renunciation, repose.

***nivṛttidharma*** (also *nivṛttimārga)* a spiritual discipline which entails the renunciation of worldly activity and involvement, including religious observances, and whose goal is withdrawal into one's deepest self or into the unmanifest.

***niyama*** rule, precept, law, vow, obligation, religious observance; the second part of Patañjali's *aṣṭaṅga yoga*, i.e. the practice of *śauca* (purity), *santoṣa* (contentment), *tapas* (austerity), *svādhyāya* (own study) and *īśvarapraṇidhāna* (self-surrender).

***nyagrodha*** the fig tree, *Ficus indica*, whose wood serves for making sacrificial bowls. It is regarded as sacred.

**Nyāya** one of the six 'orthodox' systems of Hindu philosophy which deals mainly with logic, and partly with epistemology; Navya-Nyāya: a later ('new') school within the system.

***oṁ*** (a-u-m) the sacred *mantra* called *praṇava*. Regarded as an eternal sound, it symbolizes the timeless transcendent. In its three components it represents the manifest as the time-bound triple sequence of the beginning, duration and dissolution of the universe and therefore it also stands for the three gods Brahma, Viṣṇu and Śiva. The unified sound of the *mantra* then points to the basic transcendental unity of the Trimūrti.

***padma*** lotus; a symbol of purity. Having its roots in mud, growing through water and opening its flowers to the sun in the sky make the lotus also a symbol of man's progress from the subsoil of his lower instincts and the pollutions of the saṁsāric life to the point of spiritual enlightenment. It is also used sometimes as another expression for *cakras* of the subtle body, but mainly for the seventh centre, the location of enlightenment, on top of or above the skull.

**Padmā, Padmāvatî** epithets of Lakṣmī.

**Padmanābhi** an epithet of Viṣṇu when reposing on his serpent couch floating on the cosmic waters, with a lotus growing out of his navel and Brahma sitting on the lotus.

**Padmapāṇi** an epithet of Brahma or Viṣṇu when holding a lotus in their hand (in Buddhism: a name of the Bodhisattva Avalokiteśvara).

***padmāsana*** 'lotus throne', the seat on which Brahma, Viṣṇu and Lakṣmī are often portrayed seated (as is the Buddha); lotus position, i.e. sitting cross-legged with feet resting on the opposite thighs and the soles turned upwards. It is regarded as the best position for meditation.

**Pāhlavas (Parthians)** an Iranian group of tribes. Some of them invaded India, together with Śakas (Scythians) around the turn of the era.

**Pallavas** (250–750) a South Indian dynasty which may have been started by a contingent of Pāhlavas which penetrated south and turned orthodox Hindu. Their capital was Kāñcipuram (Conjeevaram), one of the seven sacred cities of Hinduism. They built there a great Kailāsanātha temple (whose replica is the rock-carved temple in Ellorā) and the complex of Māmallapuram (Mahābalipuram).

***pañcakṣara*** a *mantra* of five syllables used by Śaivites for *japa* worship and meditation; *Namaḥ Śivāya*

***pañcama*** ('the fifth') an expression somctimes used to denote the outcast communities (officially referred to as 'scheduled classes').

***pañcamākāra*** the Tantric ritual of the five M's: *mada*, *māṁsa*, *matsya*, *mudrā* and *maithuna*; see Tantrism.

***pañcamukhaliṅga*** ('five-faced *liṅga*') a conically-shaped column with four faces carved in relief on it, usually representing various aspects of Śiva, while the fifth 'face' is invisible or represented by the *liṅga* itself, indicating that it refers to Śiva's unmanifest nature.

**Pañcarātra** a sect which originated in Kashmir (possibly in the first or second century A.D.) and whose main feature is the worship of Viṣṇu-Nārāyaṇa, with *bhakti* practice in prominence. Among its teachings is the theory of *vyūhas*, i.e. emanations of Viṣṇu, through which he manifests himself in the world with his full essential nature. This doctrine is distinct from the teaching on incarnations (*avatāras*) of Viṣṇu which it regards as lesser manifestations of the God, although it later adopted some of them and adapted them to its concept. The sect reached the peak of its popularity around the tenth century A.D. and later turned to Tantrism.

**Pāṇḍavas** one of the warring parties in the Mhb, the adversaries of the Kauravas.

**Pandit, pundit** (vern.; Skt. *paṇḍita*) a scholar learned in traditional Hindu lore.

**Pāṇini** (fifth century B.C.) author of the earliest preserved Sanskrit grammar, of a high scholarly standard, using the analytical approach and presenting a perfect system of phonetics as well as a logical alphabetical system. He is revered in Hindu tradition as a *ṛṣi*.

**Paramahaṁsa** the 'supreme swan', a symbol of the highest spiritual accomplishment; a perfectly liberated one; an honorific title for *gurus* and advanced yogis.

***paramārtha*** the highest truth; the level of the highest truth; *paramārthika*: pertaining to or concerning the level of the highest truth.

***paramātman*** the supreme self.

***paraṁ brahma*** the Supreme Brahman, the ultimate essence of reality. In Śaṅkara's Advaita Vedānta it is the sole reality identical with *paramātman*.

**Parameśvara**, ***parameśvara*** the Supreme Lord, the theistic expression for *paraṁ brahma*, the Ultimate Reality.

***paraṁparā*** uninterrupted series; oral tradition passed on for generations in direct succession from teacher to pupil.

**Paraśurāma** ('Rāma with an axe') the sixth main incarnation of Viṣṇu for the purpose of re-establishing social order disrupted by unruly clans of *kṣatriyas* and of helping brahmins to gain the upper hand over them.

***pārijāta*** the coral tree, *Erythrina indica*, which emerged from the churning of the cosmic ocean. It now grows in Indra's paradise.

***pariṣad*** a religious assembly; a group of brahmins engaged in the study of the Vedas.

***parivrājaka*** mendicant, wandering renunciate; one who has entered the fourth stage of life in the system of Hindu *āśramas* as *saṅnyāsi*.

**Parjaṇya** (Slav. Perun, Lith. Perkunas) the Vedic god of rain and storm, undoubtedly of IE descent. Of minor importance in the Vedas, because overshadowed by Rudra and Indra, he may have had a high position in the period of Brahmanism as suggested by his epithet *devarāja* (king of gods). He was the Lord of the gods in Slavonic and Baltic mythologies, on a par with the Roman Jupiter, who himself was associated with rain (cf. the Lat. saying '*Jupiter pluit*') and Gr. Zeus.

**Pārśva** the twenty-third Jain *tīrthaṅkara* who lived, according to Jain tradition, 250 years before Vardhamāna Mahāvīra.

**Pārvatī** one of the names or incarnations (as the daughter of Himavat) of Umā, the wife of Śiva. Some Śāktas see in her a form of the Goddess, a representation of *prakṛti*, and style her Jagadmātā, the mother of the universe (cf. the Vedic Aditi).

***paśu*** cattle; sacrificial animals; men in relation to gods.

**Pāśupatas** sectarian followers of Śiva with a strong devotional and humbling element. The sect was founded, according to legend, in the early second century A.D. by Lakulīśa, the author of *Pāśupatasūtra*, who is regarded by some followers of the sect as an incarnation of Śiva.

**Paśupati** ('Lord of cattle') a name of Śiva as the lord of all creatures. A Harappan icon on a seal depicting a divine figure seated cross-legged and surrounded by animals, including human figures, is widely regarded as his prototype.

***pātāla*** a name for the nether regions, seven in number, which include the realm of Nāgas (in folklore placed at the bottom of lakes and rivers) and other beings or lower deities.

**Pāṭaliputra** (modern Patna) the ancient capital of the Maurya dynasty.

**Patañjali** (possibly second century B.C.) the supposed author of the Yoga Sūtras, the earliest source of Yoga as one of the six 'orthodox' Hindu doctrines (*darśaṇas*). Nothing definite is known about him.

**Pavana** ('purifier') another name of the wind god Vāyu; sometimes used as a synonym for *prāṇa*.

**Philosophy** and philosophizing are almost inseparable from Hindu religious thought and outlook so that it is hardly possible to envisage traditional Indian philosophy as an independent subject uninvolved in religious teachings aiming at salvation, except in its formal branches such as logic and epistemology. But even in them one can detect as their ultimate concern the practical goal of final liberation.

**Pilgrimage** (*yātra*, i.e. 'going') to a sacred place (*tīrtha* - ford, crossing-point over the stream of *saṁsāra* to the other shore of salvation) is one of the most important duties or aspirations of a Hindu to be undergone at least once in one's lifetime. In the Vedic time the cult was mobile and the 'crossing-point' to higher worlds was wherever a Vedic altar was erected. In the epic time, however, pilgrimage was already fully established as a developed institution: the Mbh even describes a pilgrim's 'grand tour' which starts with Puṣkara, sacred to Brahma. Brahma's cult was contemporary with early Buddhism which itself recommends to its followers, through the mouth of the Buddha as described in the Pāli Canon, that they should go on pilgrimage to the four sacred places associated with the life of the Buddha, and therefore Buddhist influence in introducing the institution of pilgrimages into Hinduism may be inferred. Dying on pilgrimage represents, for a believing Hindu, the immediate crossing over to heaven or even salvation. Most places of pilgrimage are associated with legendary events from the lives of various gods, especially high gods and their incarnations. Almost any place can become a focus for pilgrimage, but in most cases they are sacred cities, rivers, lakes and mountains.

***piṇḍa*** regular offering to ancestors, performed also during funerals and consisting usually of rice and flour formed into balls, in Buddhism: almsfood given to monks.

***piṅgalā*** the right-hand channel (*nāḍī*) conducting *prāṇa* in the subtle body (*sukṣma śarīra*) in the system of Kuṇḍalinī Yoga.

***pippala*** the sacred fig tree, *Ficus religiosa*.

***piśāca***, f. *piśācī* evil spirit, malignant being, fiend; in popular folklore: a category of demons congregating in burial grounds and living on human flesh.

**Piśāca** the name of a tribal people.

***pitar*** father; ancestor.

***pitṛloka*** the temporary abode of deceased ancestors, sometimes identified with *svarga* (heaven) or with Yamaloka. They live there as long as their merits last, supported also by offerings made on their behalf by their descendants on earth, later to die again and be reborn in the world.

***pitṛyāna*** the mythical way of the ancestors (known also in Iranian tradition) from *pitṛloka* towards successive rebirths via the sublunar sphere, rain, plant life, animal life and back to the human state.

**Poison** (*viṣa*) the scum produced during the churning of the cosmic ocean and drunk by Śiva who thus became Nīlakaṇṭha (Bluethroat). A remnant of the poison was drunk by the serpent Vāsuki and the fumes from it were absorbed by vegetation. As a result some snakes and plants are poisonous.

**Pole ceremony** (*dhvajāropana*, 'pole planting'; cf. European Maypole erection festivals) used to be an important Hindu religious folk festival celebrated by dancing around thc pole and by courting games on the first day of the bright half of the lunar month Caitra (March/April), which is the new moon day before the spring equinox. Remnants of it survive in the Holī festival.

**Polygamy** was current in higher classes of Hindu society until the time of modern reforms under European influence.

***pradakṣiṇā*** circumambulation as a part of worship, reverence or respect, done clockwise round sacred trees, shrines, altars, monuments or temples.

**Prajāpati** 'the lord of progeny', one of the Vedic demiurge deities, later regarded as the forefather of all beings.

***prajñā*** intelligence; wisdom; the highest knowledge gained by yogic insight; the state of enlightenment; *prajñānam brahma* (*brahman* is wisdom, AU 3,3,) is one of the many additional great pronouncements (*mahāvākyas*) - besides the four main ones - which is important for the understanding of the high spiritual nature ascribed to the impersonal or suprapersonal Absolute of the Upaniṣads.

***prakaraṇa*** treatise.

**Prakrit** (*prākṛta*: natural as against *saṁskṛta*: artful, artificial) - dialect, a colloquial form of Sanskrit. Prakrits differed from province to province and there were also further variations according to class or caste. They were predecessors of modern Indian vernaculars via the Apabhraṁśa stage.

***prakṛti*** nature; cosmic manifestation; the primeval creative force responsible for the manifestation of the living universe through the interplay of its three constituent energies or *guṇas*; the second eternal principle in the dualistic system of Sāṅkhya; the 'eternal feminine' principle often identified with *māyā* and *śakti* and also with the Goddess.

***pralaya*** dissolution; the 'cosmic night' equal to a Brahma's night, the period of the dissolution of the universe at the end of a world period or *kalpa* prior to a new manifestation.

***prāṇa*** breath, breath of the gods, breath of life; life-force, the universal force which sustains all life, believed to reach the earth world with the sunlight, to enter the human body with the breath and to circulate through the *nāḍīs* of the subtle body. It is believed to be absorbed in an enhanced way during the morning *pūjā*, while reciting Gāyatrī Mantra, and when performing Surya Namaskār.

***prāṇamaya kośa*** ('sheath made of life force') a Vedāntic term for the 'vital' or subtle (also 'astral') body in the system of five sheaths, the other four *kośas* being: *annamaya*, *manomaya*, *vijñānamaya* and *ānandamaya*.

***praṇava*** (from the Vedic root *nu*, 'to sound', hence 'primeval sound') the designation for the sacred syllable *om*.

***prāṇāyama*** the control of the life force through regulated or relaxed breathing, one of the *aṅgas* in Patañjali's *aṣṭaṅga yoga*; in Hatha Yoga and Kuṇḍalinī Yoga it is an elaborate system of breathing exercises aiming at the achievement of bodily and mental health and at inducing special abilities and powers.

***praṇidhāna*** prostration, surrender, devotion.

***prasād(a)*** favour, kindness, grace; gift of gods; the portion of a consecrated offering returned to worshippers. It is usually in the form of food, shared between them.

***prasthānatrayā*** ('triple foundation') the three authoritative sources of higher knowledge recognized in the Advaita tradition, namely the early Upaniṣads, BS and the BhG. Only the Upaniṣads, though, belong to the recognized set of sacred scriptures of Hinduism.

***pratyāhāra*** (sense-)withdrawal, one of the *aṅgas* in Patañjali's *aṣṭaṅga yoga*, meaning the withdrawal of one's attention from sensory perception of external objects and their mental images and the process of focussing it inward as a preparation for inner perception.

***pratyakṣa*** perception, apprehension by the senses; common view; lower understanding (also understanding by merely logical, conceptual or intellectual means).

***pravṛtti*** rise, origin, flow, manifestation, action, continuation.

***pravṛttidharma, pravṛttimārga*** a way of action (which may involve rituals) as a means of progress on the path; a discipline of spiritual endeavour which involves continued active engagement in the world process on ever higher levels.

**Prayāga** (vern. Prag) one of the seven sacred cities of Hinduism of ancient origin, on the confluence of three rivers (*triveṇīsaṅga*): Gaṅgā, Yamunā and the invisible (mythical) river Sarasvatī. It is reputed that this was the place of Brahma's first sacrifice. It is in addition one of the four places where some drops of *amṛta*, the drink of immortality churned out of the cosmic ocean, fell when gods and *asuras* fought over it, which is commemorated by the Kuṁbha Mela festival held here once in twelve years. As the foremost place of pilgrimage it has the title *tīrtharāja*. There is an Aśokan pillar brought here from Kauśambi probably by Firoz Shāh Tughlaq, and a sacred 'undecaying' fig tree (*akṣaya-vaṭa*), both now within the fort founded by Akbar in 1581. The official name of the new town which was founded by the Mughals is Allāhābād, but it is referred to by Hindus usually as Ilāhābād, which is explained as a corruption of the name of the ancient settlement of Ilāvāsa, the abode of Ilā, the mother of an early local king from the Solar dynasty.

***prem(a)*** love; ideal love; quiet devotional affection for God without the passionate element often accompanying *bhakti*.

***preta*** a deceased one, a discarnate spirit who may linger for a time around the place of his former home before passing on to undergo the judgment of Yama (or of the guardians of *karma*), to be reborn according to merit.

***pretaloka*** the temporary abode of deceased beings in which they dwell, according to some sources, for a year until all traditional *śrāddha* ceremonies are completed. They then move on to other spheres.

***pṛthivī*** 'the broad one', the earth.

**Pṛthivī Mātar** Mother Earth as the goddess who nurtures creatures (in the Vedas the consort of Dyauḥ Pitar, the Heavenly Father)

***pūjā*** ritual worship; worship ritual.

***puṇḍarīka*** white lotus; symbol of purity; symbol of the manifested world; in Tantrism: symbol of *yoni*.

**Purāṇas** ('stories of old') religious works of Hinduism, mostly in verses, which contain legendary and mythological versions of creation, history and destruction of the universe with its divine, human and subhuman inhabitants, sometimes in great detail and dramatic narration. Some have a strong theistic tendency and sectarian character. They also popularize the idea of Trimūrti or the Hindu Trinity of Brahma, Viṣṇu and Śiva as the three aspects of one God or of the transcendental divine source when it manifests. They can be dated from the second century A.D. onwards, but contain elements of myths and legends going back to early Vedic times. There are eighteen great Purāṇas (and an equal number of auxiliary works called Upapurāṇas). The chief ones are: Brahma, Viṣṇu, Bhāgavata, Śiva, Liṅga, Vayu and Mārkaṇḍeya Purāṇas.

**Purification** (*śodhana*) is an important concept and practice in Hinduism on several levels: (1) ritual purification is necessary if caste regulations have been broken and before important *pūjās*; (2) physical purification is done both externally as a part of one's daily religious duty and more elaborately on some religious occasions, and internally by some types of *sādhus* and as a Hatha Yoga procedure; (3) psychical or 'subtly biological' purification means clearing the *nāḍis* in the subtle body by Hatha Yoga practices which involves *prāṇāyama* procedures; (4) spiritual purification requires moral discipline (such as Patañjali's *yama* and *niyama*) and the freeing of the mind from worldly concerns by meditational techniques.

***pūrṇa*** full, whole.

***pūrṇāvatāra*** a 'full' or complete incarnation of God as against a partial one. Sometimes the ten main incarnations of Viṣṇu are regarded as full, while some followers of Kṛṣṇa claim this status for him alone (apart from those who regard Kṛṣṇa as the Supreme Lord in his own right).

**Pūrṇa Yoga** integral yoga, a modern term coined by Aurobindo for his global approach to yoga practice.

***purohita*** royal chaplain; the high priest at a king's court, such as Kautilya was to Chandragupta Maurya.

***puruṣa*** person, spirit, 'soul'; the individual spiritual core of personality; in the RV (10,90) he is the primeval spiritual and person-like reality, the Absolute, and the cosmogonic source from one quarter of whom the whole manifestation emerged through the process of a cosmic sacrifice, while the other three quarters remained transcendent. (This represents one of the several Vedic myths of creation.) In the dualistic Sāṅkhya system he is the spirit representing the higher principle, the lower one being *prakṛti* (nature), but he is not there a unitary principle, being rather multiple: there is an uncounted plurality of individual *puruṣas* or eternal spirits in the universe whose exact nature is not fully explained, as it is believed to be beyond intellectual grasp. In popular epical philosophy, however, the individual *puruṣas* are regarded in the Vedāntic manner as originating from one cosmic Puruṣa or *ātman*.

***puruṣārthas*** four personal aims to be realized or striven for in the life of a Hindu, namely (1) *dharma* (duty, morality), (2) *artha* (wealth, prosperity, reputation or fame), (3) *kāma* (sensory and aesthetic fulfilment) and (4) *mokṣa* (liberation, salvation).

***puruṣottama*** 'the highest person', a perfect saint; Puruṣotama: the Supreme Lord, God (used mainly in the Vaiṣṇava context).

**Pūrva Mīmāṁsā** ('original investigation') one of the six schools of 'orthodox' Hindu thought. It developed from speculations about the parallelism between cosmic processes and ritual action which go back to very early Vedic times and are much reflected on in the Āraṇyakas and Brāhmaṇas. The system regards the Vedas as eternal and uncreated and believes that if all preliminary disciplines and set rules are observed, correct ritual action brings about guaranteed results, including salvation.

**Pūṣan** (nourisher) a Vedic god, associated with fertility, marriage rites and childbirth, the bringer of prosperity and well-being. He is later associated with the Sun as deity.

***puṣkara*** blue lotus; Brahma's lotus throne; an epithet of Śiva and also of Kṛṣṇa.

**Puṣpaka** a palatial aerial car, a gift of Brahma to Kubera which was stolen from him by Rāvaṇa and recovered for him by Rāma after Rāvaṇa's defeat.

**Rādha** a *gopi*, the wife of the cowherd Ayanaghoṣa in Vṛndāvana and the favourite sweetheart of Kṛṣṇa, regarded by his devotees as his *śakti* and also as an incarnation of Lakṣmī. Another view of her is that she is an embodiment of the mystic love of the human soul for god.

***rāga*** desire; emotion; a musical form or mode expressing emotion. *Rāgas* are classified according to the time of day or night whose mood they are supposed to express.

**Rāhu** ('seizer') a lunar deity; a demon responsible for the eclipses of the moon and sun by swallowing them. He became immortal by stealing and drinking some of the *amṛta* churned from the cosmic ocean.

**Raidās** (Ravidās, also: Rohidās; fifteenth century) a disciple of Rāmānanda and the reputed teacher of Mīrā-bāī, the famous Vaiṣṇava poetess and saint.

***rāja*** chief, chieftain, prince, king, sovereign (cf. Lat. *rex*); in ancient times he also had a certain priestly status which was later replaced by kingship with divine sanction conferred on him during the consecration ceremony carried out by the high priest.

***rājarṣi*** a seer or saint of royal or *kṣatriya* descent.

***rajas*** passion; energy; one of the three *guṇas* (dynamic forces) of *prakṛti*, the other two being *sattva* (purity) and *tamas* (inertia).

***rājasūya*** the ceremonial consecration of the king performed by the *purohita* and assisted by the representatives of the three higher or 'twice-born' castes. During it the king assumed an elevated position standing with arms stretched upwards in imitation of the cosmic tree and the cosmic pillar connecting heaven and earth, thereby indicating the source of his authority.

**Rāja Yoga** a medieval term coined to stress the higher status of meditational yoga practice over the physical aspects of the Hatha Yoga practices.

**Rājputs** ruling *kṣatriya* clans of Rājputana (now Rājasthan). Most of them were probably descended from invading warrior groups prior to and during the Gupta time and some from indigenous hinduized tribes of warrior character who rose to prominence in post-imperial time. All of them wholeheartedly embraced the Hindu tradition and claimed to be of ancient Āryan origin, which they expressed usually mythologically by deriving their descent from Solar and Lunar dynasties of the Purāṇas. They played an important part in the fight against Muslim invaders, but in the Mughal time some of them were won over to serve the emperors, while others continued with their relentless resistance.

***rākṣasa*** a category of demons or malignant spirits inimical to man, appearing in various, often animal, forms and roaming at night; a derogatory epithet for jungle tribes.

**Rāma, Rāmacandra** a prince from the reigning family in the ancient city of Ayodhyā, the hero of the epic Rāmāyaṇa, who came to be regarded as the seventh main incarnation of Viṣṇu. Rāma's bridge (called Adam's Bridge on modern maps) is the line of little islands between India and Sri Lanka which are said to be the remnants of the bridge built by Hanumān's troops to cross over to rescue Sītā.

**Ramakrishna** (1836–86) a Bengali brahmin, most of his life settled as the priest of the goddess Kālī in her temple in Dakṣineśvar, Calcutta, who gained the reputation of a saint, a realized mystic and a yogi accomplished in *bhakti* as well as *jñāna* systems. He had a vision of Kṛṣṇa at the age of thirty-five when he was impersonating Rādhā and he also tried Christian and Muslim mystic approaches and claimed to have had visions of Christ and of a Muslim saint. He concluded that all religions provided a path to God, but he himself remained the life-long devotee of Mother Kālī, his *iṣṭa devatā*. The world-wide organization 'Ramakrishna Math Mission' founded after his death is still active both in India and abroad and propagates a popular form of Advaitism, besides social, educational and general cultural activities.

**Ramaṇa Maharṣi** (1879–1950) one of the first Hindu yogis with a world-wide reputation, born in South India. Diverted from his studies at the age of sixteen by a sudden spiritual experience of his undying inner self, he left home and settled at the foot of the hill Arunachala near Tiruvannamalai where an *āśram* grew around him within a few years and where he lived for the rest of his life. Among his admirers and visitors, who all invariably testified to the genuine impression he made on them, were also high-ranking politicians and academics. His many followers adopted his 'inquiring method' of meditational search for the inner self, which can be characterized as a type of Jñāna Yoga steeped in Advaitic tradition, but his presentation of it was simple and straightforward.

**Rāmānanda** (fourteenth to fifteenth century A.D.) the fifth successive leader and teacher of the Viśiṣṭa Advaita school of thought, founded by Rāmānuja, and a prominent *bhakta*. He later founded his own sect and wrote *bhajans*, devotional hymns, in Hindi.

**Rāmānuja** (eleventh to twelfth century A.D.) the founder of the Vedāntic school of thought known as 'qualified non-dualism

(Viśiṣṭa Advaita). He was born near Madrās and came from the Pañcarātra tradition. He wandered India as a *saṅnyāsi* for a time and eventually settled in Śriraṅga from where he only temporarily fled to avoid forceful conversion to Śaivism by the Chola king. He taught that the Upaniṣadic *brahman* was at the same time the transcendental divine source and also the highest personal God, namely Viṣṇu. According to him, God possesses, as well as his spiritual nature, a subtle body and by transforming it into a gross one, he brought about the creation of the world. The individual, while being in a way himself, is in essence only God's attribute and can reach his *mokṣa* on the path of *bhakti* by getting to know God, i.e. by apprehending him in a kind of cognitive mystic union. Rāmānuja wrote extensive commentaries on the Upaniṣads, the BS and the BhG. His sectarian followers hold him for an incarnation of Viṣṇu's serpent Śeṣa/Ananta.

**Rāmāyaṇa** the story of Rāma and his wife Sītā as they went into exile, accompanied by Rāma's brother Lakṣmaṇa, and of how Sītā was abducted by Rāvaṇa, the demon-king of Laṅkā, and rescued with the help of Hanumān, the king of the monkey tribes. It is the earliest Indian epic, composed in 24000 *ślokas*, reputedly by Vālmīki, but obviously a composite work the bulk of which is dated by some to around 500 B.C., by others to 300 B.C., with subsequent extensions added up to A.D. 200–300.

**Rāmeśvara** a city and place of pilgrimage with a temple sacred to Rāma on an island just off the coast and connected to it, at the Indian end of the so-called Rāma's bridge.

**Rāmlīlā** (Rāma's sporting) a dramatic enactment of the story of Rāma's life during the Daṣahrā festival in some parts of North India, lasting several days and based on the adaptation of the epic Rāmāyaṇa, called *Rāmcaritmānas*, by Tulsīdās (cca 1543–1623).

***raṇgāvalī*** (vern. *raṅgoli)* a form of *yantra* in popular use in South India, meant to welcome guests and friendly deities, drawn by women in front of their houses after cleaning the house as part of their housework.

***rasa*** sap, juice, elixir, essence, semen; taste; inclination, desire, affection, love; feeling, sentiment, emotion, pathos; in poetic compositions: aesthetic sentiment (usually eight kinds are recognized, and to them is added *śānta* – tranquillity).

***rāsa*** a circular dance round a fixed centre. Kṛṣṇa performed it with *gopīs*, whirling round from one partner to another so quickly that none of them noticed his absence and each one of them experienced his presence without interruption. This sometimes tends to be interpreted as a symbol of God's continuous communion with the soul in the *bhakti* relationship, which is undiminished by the multiplicity of souls.

**Rāstrakūta** (750–973) a dynasty prominent in West Deccan, probably originating from an ennobled indigenous clan. They were great art patrons responsible for some cave temples and the Kailāsa rock temple of Ellorā and possibly also for the Elephanta rock-carved temple complex.

***rati*** pleasure, aesthetic pleasure, delight; attachment to, fondness for, devotion to, love.

**Rati** the wife of Kāma, the god of love.

**Rāvaṇa** the demon-king of Laṅkā in the epic Rāmayaṇa, half-brother of Kubera. He abducted Sītā and was defeated and killed in the fight for her recovery.

***ṛg, ṛc*** verse.

**Ṛg Veda** ('knowledge in verses') the first Vedic collection of 1028 hymns codified around 1000 B.C. It is the oldest preserved religious book known to mankind. It contains several mythological and poetical accounts of the origin of the world as well as attempts to explain it philosophically, cryptic references to many mythological stories and legends in existence at the time, hymns of praise directed to the gods, some of them of great lyrical beauty, indications of the search for immortality and of a path to it found by legendary ancient *ṛṣis*, prayers for long life and prosperity etc.

**Ritual** (*kriyā, karman*) a symbolical procedure believed to reflect cosmic and spiritual processes to which individuals and communities are linked or subjected and which they can influence through it. There is a rite for each stage of a Hindu's life, from conception and birth to cremation, as well as for departed ancestors, and there are communal rituals for important periods during the year, while state rituals, formerly associated with kingship, have been largely abandoned. In a more formal sense, ritual is believed to establish channels of communication and exchange of values between men and the gods or God.

**Rivers** are regarded as sacred in Hinduism and are addressed as deities, usually goddesses but in a few cases gods, just as in other IE mythologies.

**Roy, Rājā Rām Mohan** (1772–1833) a Hindu reformer and founder of Brahma Sabhā (1828), later changed to Brāhmo Samāj. He was born into a high caste brahmin family of Caitanya followers and educated in Patna where he experienced some Islamic influences. He then became acquainted with Christianity and Western liberal ideas through his friendship with Christian missionaries and while he worked for the East India Company. He later embarked on study of the Upaniṣads and Vedāntic philosophy and as a result of all these influences he developed a reformist view of Hinduism. He fought against child marriage and campaigned against the burning of widows (*satī*), thus facilitating the outlawing of the custom by Lord Bentinck, the governor-general, in 1829. He founded his organization under the influence of European Unitarianism and introduced into it a congregational type of worship unknown in mainstream Hinduism. He rejected castes, priesthood, sacrifice and images of God and also the teaching of transmigration. He died in Bristol while on a journey to Europe.

***ṛṣi*** seer. This term was originally used only for the inspired composers of at least one Ṛgvedic hymn, but later it came to be applied also to some Upaniṣadic and other types of sages, such as the seven *ṛṣis* of the Purāṇas. In the extended form as *maharṣi* (maharishi, great seer) the term has been used (and misused) in later and modern times as an honorific title for (and by) various types of *sādhus* and *gurus*.

***ṛta*** right; truth; the cosmic law of balance governing the cosmic processes: natural, social, moral and spiritual. It is a Vedic expression which went out of use, its principles being preserved in post-Vedic times by the notions of (*sanātana*) *dharma* and *karma*.

***ṛtu*** a point in time; a precise time appointed for a sacrifice (according to astrological calculations and traditional rules).

***ṛtvij*** a priest as the performer of sacrificial rites.

**Rudra** ('howler') the Vedic god of storms, accompanied by Maruts, the bringer of destruction. However, he is also, on occasions, known as a healer who can be gracious (*śiva*, in post-Vedic time adopted as his main name) and even act as a saviour: the Purāṇic myth about his act of drinking the poison to save creation from destruction is already alluded to in the RV 10,136,7 and his blue throat resulting from it is mentioned in the YV (VS 16,7).

**Rukmiṇī** the principal wife of Kṛṣṇa, who abducted her on the day of her wedding to another man. She is often regarded as an incarnation of Lakṣmī.

***rūpa*** shape, form; bodily form; material body; figure; image of god (also of the Buddha and Jina).

***saccidānanda*** (*sat-cit-ānanda*) existence-consciousness-bliss, the Advaitic expression for the ultimate reality or experience thereof. Despite the triple expression, it is maintained that the experience itself is one of unification. That means that these three phenomenologically distinct concepts are nevertheless regarded not as separate entities or qualities of the ultimate reality, but as representing the unity of its spiritual essence.

**Sacraments** (*saṁskāras*) rituals which mark the chief phases in the life of a Hindu, the most important ones being conception, birth, name-giving, marriage and the funeral (cremation).

**Sacred thread** a mark of belonging to one of the three higher castes worn on the naked body across the left shoulder. It is bestowed on male youngsters at the initiation ceremony regarded as the 'second birth' which makes them full members of their caste, and in ancient times it marked the beginning of their status as *brahmacāris*. The custom goes back to Indo-Iranian times, but today it is observed mainly by brahmins.

**Sacrifice** (*yajña*) the ritual enactment of mutuality (or of the 'give and take' relation) between the individual and the universe (God or gods), i.e. the recognition that man depends on the universal force or forces for his well-being and that the state of the universe depends on the attitudes, concerns and actions of man. The cosmic dimension of sacrifice and its link to the process of creation is expressed in the Puruṣa Sūkta (RV 10,90). In the Brahminical orthodoxy ritual sacrifice was essential also for man's salvation. Higher spiritual teachings and systems favouring personal discipline and yoga re-interpreted sacrifice as sacrificing or giving up one's ego or outer personality and renouncing worldly possessions for the sake of salvation in union with the ultimate truth.

***sadguru*** true spiritual teacher; a truly competent master who can teach the right method individually on the basis of his direct insight into his pupil's mind or heart.

***sādhaka***, f. *sādhika* adept; a person striving for accomplishment.

***sādhanā*** personal spiritual discipline; a way to accomplishment.

***sādhu*** holy man, religious mendicant; often used also as an exclamation: '*sādhu, sādhu*', meaning 'it is so, holy truth'.

***saguṇa brahman*** *brahman* with attributes, the divine source of reality when conceived as the first manifested entity, usually as

Brahma the creator or the highest God such as Śiva or Viṣṇu in the sectarian context.

***sahaja*** (*saha*=with, *ja*=born) a sectarian Tantric term which was coined to express the view held by Sahajiya followers that natural qualities of things and inborn characteristics and tendencies of beings belong to their ultimate innate nature and that beings are born with that nature into this world. They equate this innate nature present in every individual with the Upaniṣadic *ātman* and its ultimateness with *brahman*. But the way to full realization, in individual experience, of this ultimateness is not seen by them to lie in the elimination of the natural, inborn, innate tendencies, such as the sex-impulse. Rather one should work with them, experiencing them to the full, and through them reach the point of ecstatic transformation and salvation in the ultimate freedom of the Sahaja in their 'own body of the ultimate nature' (*svābhāvika kāya*).

**Sahajiyā cult** a medieval Tantric movement with left-handed practices wrapped in ritual. It operated across sectarian boundaries and included also Buddhist Tantrics and Bāuls, but many Sahajiyā groups had Vaiṣṇava leanings and modelled their path on the relationship of Kṛṣṇa with Rādhā.

***sahasrāra padma*** (thousand-petalled lotus) the seventh spiritual centre according to Kuṇḍalinī Yoga, placed at the top of the skull or above (in the subtle body or aura), the meeting-point of the individual and universal consciousness.

***sākṣin*** ('witness') a late Vedāntic term, used especially in the context of Jñāna Yoga, for the inner Self as the silent observer, unperturbed by external events and mental processes within the outward, phenomenal personality.

***samādhi*** concentration; unification; deep meditative absorption in some yoga systems, including Patañjali's (the eighth limb), regarded as a state of higher cognition; also: tomb of a *guru*.

***sāman*** song, chant, song of praise.

**Sāma Veda** ('knowledge in songs') the second Vedic collection, compiled around 900–800 B.C., almost exclusively from the hymns of the RV, for liturgical use.

***saṁhitā*** collection; a volume of hymns or treatises.

***sampradāya*** teacher-pupil succession; handing down of tradition; sectarian tradition.

***saṁsāra*** ('global flow') the individual round of rebirths within the various cosmic planes of existence determined by the law of *karma*; the global flow of manifested reality, periodically renewed in cycles of world absorption and new manifestation.

***sanātana*** everlasting.

**Sanātana Dharma** (eternal truth or law) a term for the central teaching of Hinduism about the continuous cyclic returns of the manifestation of the universe and of the beings within it under the all-pervading cosmic law. Cf. Cosmogony, Creation, *karma*, *ṛta*, Transmigration, and the Introduction.

**Sanatkumāra** ('eternal youth') the designation of Brahma when he appears to lower beings in the shape of a beautiful youngster; the name of Brahma's son; a title sometimes used for accomplished ascetics.

***sāṅkhya*** enumeration; discrimination; deliberation; investigation.

**Sāṅkhya** one of the six Hindu systems of philosophy, traditionally ascribed to Kapila (cca 500 B.C.) as its founder. It is dualistic in that it recognizes two eternal principles, namely *puruṣa* (spirit) and *prakṛti* (nature), and pluralistic in that it accepts a multiplicity of eternal *puruṣas*. *Prakṛti*, using her three creative potencies or *guṇas*, conjures up the world process for the benefit of *puruṣas* and creates for them material bodies, senses and mental functions, virtually creating for them prakṛtic, phenomenal or worldly personalities. The *puruṣas* are at first inactive observers of these displays of *prakṛti*, but get carried away by them and identify with their prakṛtic bodily forms, their sensory and mental experiences and their roles in the events in worldly life, forgetting their true status. When a *puruṣa* recognizes his situation for what it is, namely an irksome entanglement depriving him of his freedom, he can initiate the process of his liberation from it by mentally discriminating between all prakṛtic evolutes or formations (including all intruding sensory perceptions and mental processes) and his own pure consciousness. The *puruṣa* thereby dissociates himself from the evolutes of *prakṛti* and the whole prakṛtic universe, his prakṛtic personality dissolves and he gains total freedom, called *kaivalya*. The system does not recognize a God or lord (*īśvara*).

**Sāṅkhya-Yoga** a combination of the metaphysical teachings of the Sāṅkhya school of thought with the practice of the classical yoga path as outlined in Patañjali's Yoga Sūtras.

***saṁnyās(a)*** renunciation; a state of homelessness; a life style in renunciation, aiming at spiritual accomplishment, which may sometimes involve belonging to a monastic community; also: the fourth stage of life in the system of *āśrama dharma*.

***saṁnyāsi*** renunciate, mendicant, homeless wanderer; member of a spiritual order.

**Sanskrit** (*saṁskṛta*: composed, refined, polished, made perfect, artful, artificial) the sacred and literary language of ancient and medieval India which underwent several stages of development. Its oldest form, the language of the Vedic hymns, differs in some respects from that of the Upaniṣads, the later parts of the Veda, in ways which suggest not only normal evolution of language, but also a shift in authorship to a slightly different linguistic group. The classical form of Sanskrit was codified by Pāṇini around 500 B.C. and most of the religious and epic literature conforms more or less to his rules. It was further refined by poets in the Gupta time, while a form of Sanskrit deviating from the classical norm (and known as Buddhist Hybrid Sanskrit) started being employed for Buddhist writings around the turn of the era. Like Latin in medieval Europe, Sanskrit continued to be used by learned and priestly circles long after spoken forms of the language had developed into regional and class vernaculars, a process which started in very early times. Many priests and pandits still speak Sanskrit, which is also the medium of teaching in the Benares Sanskrit University.

***sant*** holy man; a term for *bhakta*-type holy men who do not belong to the mainstream Viṣṇuite movements, being influenced by Nātha cults and Sūfism or being active within the Sikh tradition.

***saṁtoṣa*** satisfaction, contentment; one of the *niyamas* in Patañjali's *aṣṭaṅga yoga.*

***saptamātṛkās*** a group of seven goddesses, mostly consorts of major gods, given prominence in medieval popular Hinduism and among *śakti* worshippers, and often depicted on a single icon; Brahmāṇī, Māheśvarī, Kaumārī, Vaiṣṇavī, Vārāhī, Indrāṇī and Chāmuṇḍī, sometimes with Ganeṣa in attendance. Generally they stand for the reproductive forces of nature and female fecundity.

***saptarṣi*** 'the seven seers', a group of sages referred to briefly in the RV and later writings, particularly in the Purāṇas. They are sometimes called the 'mind-born sons of Brahma', are variously named and were divinized as the seven stars of the Great Bear constellation.

**Saptasindhu** ('the land of the seven rivers') the expression known from the RV which denotes the cradle of the Vedic civilization in former Pañjāb (Punjab, the land of five rivers, now in Pakistan) to which must be added a further territory, probably marked by the upper Gaṅgā (Ganges) and Yamunā (Jumna). Some sources give differing lists of names of the seven rivers, some of them probably mythical. There is also a purely mythological list referring to mythical streams associated with the descent of Gaṅgā from heaven.

**Sarasvatī** ('the flowing one') in the Vedas just a river goddess, she gradually came to represent waters in general with their cosmic symbolism and the association with Vāc and the cosmic mind, eventually becoming the goddess of wisdom and the wife of Brahma. Her mount is mostly a swan, but sometimes a ram, an owl, a parrot or a peacock.

***sarvaṁ khalvidam brahma*** 'all this is verily *brahman*' (CU 3,14,1), one of the four 'Great Sayings' (*mahāvākyas*) of the Upaniṣads expressing the Vedāntic philosophy of oneness, widely popularized as a basic Hindu tenet.

***sat*** being, existence, reality; the first component of the compound *saccidānanda*, designating experience of the ultimate reality in the Advaita Vedānta system.

**Satavahana, Sātavāhana** (cca 100 B.C.–A.D. 200) a dynasty in the Deccan, of Āndhra origin. Early Buddhist rock-carved monasteries, important also for Hindu iconography, at Karli, West Deccan, and other Buddhist monuments, such as the stūpa at Amarāvatī, were constructed during their reign.

***satī*** wife; perfect wife; also: the designation for a faithful wife who voluntarily follows her deceased husband onto the funeral pyre. By a wrong application of the term it came to be used for the act of burning widows with their deceased husbands (anglicized as 'suttee'). The Skt. expressions for this practice were: *sahagama* ('going with'), *anugama* ('going after'), *anumaraṇa* ('dying after') and others. The practice seems to have been rare in ancient times, but it is mentioned in Gr. chronicles in the fourth century B.C. It became quite customary with *kṣatriyas* by the first century B.C., then receded, but started increasing again in the sixth century and later, especially in the wake of the Islamic invasions as a way of escaping capture and slavery. It then came to be regarded by the Brahminic establishment as an important part of their ancient tradition to be sustained under both Muslim and British rule, and instances of dubious methods of pressurizing reluctant victims to undergo the rite have been recorded. Muslim rulers tried to limit the custom and it was condemned by some Hindu poets, by Tantric writers and by various reformers. It was made illegal by the British in 1829 under Lord Bentinck, but isolated cases continued to be recorded from time to time, one as late as 1946. Cases of attempted revival of the practice were recorded newly in the 1980s. Some IE evidence for the antiquity of the rite is furnished by Nordic mythology (from where it probably got into the last act of Wagner's *Götterdämmerung*).

**Satī** the daughter of Dakṣa who chose Śiva for her husband at her *svayaṁvara* against her father's wishes. When, according to Purāṇic mythology, her father later offended Śiva, she burned herself to death in protest, was reborn as Umā and again became Śiva's wife.

***satsaṅg(a)*** ('intercourse with true reality') a religious gathering headed by or centred around a reputed spiritual personality.

***sattva*** being, entity, essence; purity; goodness; truth; reality; lucidity, one of the three *guṇas* (dynamic forces) of *prakṛti*, the other two being *rajas* (energy) and *tamas* (inertia).

***satya*** truth; truthfulness; one of the *yamas* of Patañjali's *aṣṭaṅga yoga*.

***savikalpa samādhi*** a term used in Jñāna Yoga for a deep state of meditational absorption in which the subject-object dichotomy is still experienced, but understood directly as unsubstantial.

**Savitar** a Vedic solar god, the 'brilliant' one, the golden sun, the lord of vivifying, life-sustaining power to whom is addressed the daily invocation from the RV 3,62,10 known as Sāvitrī or, more commonly, Gāyatrī Mantra.

**Sāyana** (fourteenth century) a notable commentator on the RV who lived in Vijayanagar, the last Hindu kingdom to resist the Islamic sovereignty.

**Science** in ancient India was advanced in some branches. The decimal numerical system reached Europe from India by Arabic mediation and, generally speaking, European mathematics overtook Indian achievements only with Leibniz. Astronomical notions concerning the enormous size and extremely long duration of the universe and the multiplicity of world systems also preceded by many centuries the European grasp of such matters.

While its outlook remains naturally supramundane, contemporary Hinduism has a positive attitude to modern scientific knowledge and accommodates it without any problems as long as science confines itself to its own subject area and does not overstep the mark by insisting on denying transcendental levels of reality and the validity of the cosmic law in all its spheres, including its spiritual and moral dimensions.

**Script** appeared in India from about eighth or seventh century B.C., was called *brāhmī* and was derived from proto-Semitic sources, probably as a result of commercial contacts with Mesopotamian countries. Aśoka used it in his rock edicts. From the fifth or fourth century B.C. another script appeared called *kharoṣṭhī*, also based on a Semitic example, and after a process of modification the *nāgarī* or *devanāgarī* script emerged which was widely used by the time of the Guptas. Its earliest known examples are from the eighth century A.D. and it was perfected by the eleventh century into the form still in use for Sanskrit texts and for modern Hindī.

**Scriptures** strictly speaking they are represented solely by the Veda which is regarded as revelation (*śruti*) and includes the four Vedas, the Brāhmaṇas and the Upaniṣads. However, great authority, almost matching that of the Upaniṣads, is ascribed to the BhG, which is a part of the epic literature (*itihāsa*), but has the authority of a scripture in the eyes of many Hindus. Sectarian movements also regard their particular texts, such as Āgamas and even Purāṇas, as revealed scriptures, but these are not recognized as such in mainstream Hinduism.

**Self** (*ātman*) besides being a reflexive pronoun which may refer to any constituent or layer of the human personality, it refers in the context of Hindu thought predominantly to the elusive innermost core of one's being which can be experienced only as a result of the highest spiritual achievement.

**Sen, Keshab Chandra** (1838–84) a Hindu reformer who worked first within Brāhmo Samāj, but later went his own separate way. He preached the fatherhood of God and the brotherhood of man and supported ecumenism. In later years he turned to syncretic mysticism, mixing Christian and Hindu imagery and rituals.

**Seven sacred cities of Hinduism** are: (1) Ayodhyā, the birthplace of Rāma; (2) Mathurā, the birthplace of Kṛṣṇa; (3) Haridvāra (Hardwār) where Gaṅgā descends from the mountains and enters the plain of North India; (4) Gayā, sacred to Viṣṇu; (5) Varāṇasī (Kāśī), the city of Śiva; (6) Prayāga, at the confluence of Gaṅgā, Yamunā and the invisible Sarasvatī; and (7) Dvārakā, the capital of Kṛṣṇa's kingdom.

**Shanti Sadan** a London centre of Vedāntic studies and practice (under the name of Adhyatma Yoga), one of the first in the West, founded in 1929 by Dr. Hari Prasad Shastri, an academic scholar as well as a traditional spiritual teacher (*ācārya*).

***siddha*** a perfect (liberated) person; a term preferred in some Tantric schools for their accomplished masters possessed of great paranormal powers. Often referred to as Mahāsiddhas and reckoned to be 84 in number, they were regarded as immortal in their bodies and were greatly revered. The popular Siddha cult recognized 88,000 of them and placed their abode in the intermediate region between the terrestrial and heavenly worlds.

***siddhi*** accomplishment, perfection; magic power gained on a path of spiritual progress or yoga. Magic powers are usually purposely sought by Tantrics, but some schools of yoga regard them as an undesirable and potentially dangerous by-product which, acquired before full accomplishment, may lead the aspirant astray.

**Sikhism** a monotheistic religion which rejects most of the tenets of Hinduism, but teaches rebirth and liberation through the spiritual path and also accepts yoga practice. It was founded by Guru Nānak, perhaps as an alternative to Hinduism and Islam, and developed under subsequent leaders, also referred to as Gurus, into a well-organized community and military power fighting the Mughals. After the decline of the Mughal rule, the Sikhs founded their own state and at one time dominated a large part of North West India, but lost it to the British power. In recent years a militant section within the Sikh movement has embarked on a struggle, at times armed, for the re-establishment of an independent Sikh state carved out of the territory of the Indian republic, although the largest part of the traditional Sikh domain is now in Pakistan, from which most Sikhs were driven during the partition and found refuge and new life in the Indian republic where they have prospered.

***siṁha*** lion; used as a symbol of strength and sovereignty, both worldly and spiritual, in names and also as a title.

**Sin** a concept which does not have a full equivalent in Hinduism; one speaks rather of evil deeds committed out of ignorance of their karmic consequences. Brahminic orthodoxy recognizes also a concept of ritual evil or pollution.

**Sītā** ('furrow') a goddess in the RV, ruling fields and orchards. Her festival was the ceremonial ploughing of the first furrow in the spring done by the *rāja*. Also: the name of Rāma's wife, who is still revered as an embodiment of female chastity and marital fidelity. Born from a furrow, she is called Ayonija ('one not born from a womb') and is regarded as an incarnation of Lakṣmī.

***skaṁbha***, Skaṁbha, also: *staṁbha* pillar; the pole which represents the cosmic prop of creation holding apart heaven and earth; the axis of the universe connecting the material world with the spiritual worlds and ultimately with the centre or essence of reality, i.e. *brahman*/*ātman* (Cf. RV 8,41; AV 10,7; 10,8). This ancient idea is symbolically present in some creation myths, fertility rites and festivals and temple structures, as e.g. in Indra's spear used in his combat with Vṛtra, in the sacrificial pole and in the flagpole of Indian temples as well as their *śikharas*, in Aśokan pillars and other votive poles, in *liṅga* worship and village festive *rāsa* dances round a pole (still known even in European folklore as maypole dancing) etc.

**Skanda** god of war, see Kārttikeya.

***smārta*, Smārta** based on tradition, based on Smṛtis.

***smṛti*, Smṛti** that which is remembered; tradition; a summary designation of scriptures which do not have the status of revelation (*śruti*, that which was heard, i.e. revealed), but possess great religious authority. They are: the auxiliary Vedic sciences known as Vedāṅgas; Smārta Sūtras; Dharmaśāstras; Itihāsa, including the epics, the Purāṇas and the Upapurāṇas; and Nītiśāstras (ethical and didactic writings, including fables).

***soma*** (Av. *haoma*) a plant regarded as sacred whose juice, which had intoxicating effects, was used in Vedic times for ritual purposes. Its preparation was itself a ritual and involved pressing it and adding to its juice water, milk, butter and barley. The actual plant used may have changed with availability of plants in the course of migrations and its identification is still a subject of controversy. Symbolically: divine ecstasy, mystic experience, enlightenment; in later mythology it refers also to *amṛta*, the drink of immortality, stored in the moon which wanes when gods drink it and waxes when it automatically refills.

**Soma** the Moon god and guardian of herbs who rides in a car drawn by antelopes or in a three-wheeled chariot drawn by ten white horses. He once abducted for a time Tārā, the wife of Bṛhaspati, and as a result she gave birth to Budha (the planet Mercury).

**Soul** there is no precise equivalent of this notion in Hinduism, if we understand it as an indestructible individual substance created by God at a certain point of time, but for eternity. Different Hindu schools have different conceptions of what is in Western languages called soul and employ different expressions for it, but generally speaking, the 'soul' which transmigrates from life to life is understood to be a complex personality structure, composed of several layers or 'sheaths' or subtle 'bodies', which may harbour a universal core which is common to all but remains untouched by its relation to the multiplicity of persons just as the moon is not touched by its multiple reflections in waters. There is also a variety of conceptions of the 'soul' in the state of liberation, from complete merging with the universal core (the *brahman* of the Advaita Vedānta school) to total individual independence (the *puruṣa* of the Sāṅkhya system).

***sṛṣṭi*** ('sending forth') emanation, manifestation; often also translated as 'creation', but it must be borne in mind that this never means creation out of nothing, but stands for a re-emergence of the world from the state of latency after a cosmic period of rest.

***staṁbha*** see *skaṁbha.*

**Stūpa** burial mound; a Buddhist relic mound, a place of worship and symbol of the Buddha's entry into *nirvāṇa*. Originally stūpas were fairly simple circular mounds with a ring of stones round them. Those with interred relics of kings and war heroes tended to become embellished and more firmly constructed. According to Buddhist sources the relics of the Buddha's body after burning were divided into eight portions and buried in various parts of the country in stūpas, which then became places of worship as symbols of the Buddha in the final state of *nirvāṇa*. It is believed that Aśoka had the Buddha's relics taken out of some of the original stūpas, that they were then divided and that many more stūpas were built over them. Stūpas were built also over relics of saintly monks which likewise became foci of worship.

**Sūfism** a mystical movement within Islam. It originated in the Middle East in the first centuries of Islamic history from ascetic tendencies among 'seekers of God', small groups of individuals, forming independent semi-monastic communities. They were intent on finding certainty that they had escaped the threat of hell and they eventually came to see it in the achievement of the mystical experience of oneness with God. Their name comes from wearing garments of wool (*ṣūf*). They were influenced by Hellenistic, Gnostic, Christian and Indian mysticism and were often persecuted as heretics by Islamic orthodoxy. By the eleventh century Sūfism had reached India, where its pantheism (the view that God is in everything) was further strengthened by contacts with Vedāntic trends in Hinduism and in turn itself exercised profound influence on some individuals weary of Hindu orthodoxy (e.g. Kabīr), some ascetic movements (e.g. Bāuls) and some sections of the Hindu population.

***sukha*** happiness, pleasure; in the context of spiritual practice it often denotes the subtle feeling of well-being or happiness which is the result of the withdrawal of attention from the sensory perceptions and consequent unburdening of the mind from worldly preoccupations; in left-hand Tantrism it refers to the meditational experience during *maithuna* (cf. *mahāsukha*) in the state of *samādhi*.

***sūkṣma*** subtle; *sūkṣma śarīra*: subtle body, the seat of the *cakras* and other faculties according to the teachings of Kuṇḍalinī and Tantric Yoga.

***sūkta*** hymn; Vedic hymn.

**Sumeru** see Meru.

***sura*, Sura(s)** a class of solar demigods or lower deities inhabiting Indra's heaven, their name being possibly derived from *svar*. Another explanation is that they owe their 'existence' to the false etymology of the word *asura* as *a-sura* (non-*sura*) when its ancient meaning of 'high god' was largely forgotten and its meaning changed to 'anti-god' which required the existence of *suras* as a separate class of deities.

***surā*** liquor; wine; Surā: goddess of intoxicating drinks.

**Sūrya** the Vedic Sun god, the chief Āditya. Besides his obvious life-giving powers and ability to disperse darkness with his light, he also illuminates the mind, dispersing the darkness of ignorance for meditators, thus symbolizing enlightenment as expressed in the Gāyatrī Mantra and other hymns of the RV.

**Sūrya Namaskār** ('salutation to the sun') a dynamic series of exercises best performed at the time and in the direction of the rising sun. It is a part of the Hatha Yoga system.

***suṣumnā*** the central channel or *nāḍī* in the subtle body which occupies the same space as the spinal cord along which are placed the *cakras* as described in the system of Kuṇḍalinī Yoga.

***sūtra*** thread, guideline, aphorism; a literary treatise in a very condensed, aphoristic style. It may have originated in the context of oral tradition either as the notes of the teacher for his use when instructing his pupils or as notes or records of the teacher's instructions taken down by pupils. As a result most *sūtra* type works are difficult to interpret or even impossible to understand without the help of commentaries.

***svabhāva*** own nature; what a being or a thing really is.

***svadhā*** offering, oblation.

***svādhiṣṭhāna*** (self-based) *cakra* opposite the generative organs in the shape of a six-petalled lotus.

***svādhyāya*** (from *dhyai*, to think, meditate, contemplate) own study, one of the *niyamas* in Patañjali's *aṣṭaṅga yoga*.

***svāhā*** ritual exclamation during oblation; added as the last word to some *mantras*.

**Svāmi, Swami** (from Skt. *svāmi*: owner, lord, master) the honorific title of learned brahmins, *gurus* and publicly active *saṅnyāsis*.

***svapna*** sleep, sleep with dreams, dreaming.

***svar*** heaven; paradise; radiance, splendour; spiritual enlightenment.

***svarāj*** self-rule; self-government; in the spiritual sense: mastery of oneself, self-control.

***svarga*** heaven; the heaven of Indra situated on mount Meru; an existential dimension inhabited by beings reborn there for a time to reap the merits of their good deeds in blissful existence before being reborn again on earth or in other regions.

***svastika*** (fr. Skt. *su* 'well' and *asti* 'is', i.e. 'all is well') an object bringing luck, an auspicious sign. The sign popularized under this name by the Nazis is thought to have been an ancient symbol of the sun and appears in the context of Buddhism as well as Hinduism, but it was also used in ancient Near Eastern cultures. In India it is still associated with the cult of Viṣṇu and when painted on doors, it is believed to protect from the evil eye.

***svayaṁbhū*** self-existent; not created or not dependent for existence on another agent or anything else. This term applies to the Upaniṣadic *brahman* as the self-existent transcendent divine source of all manifested existence and was used in the Upaniṣads as an epithet of the Lord (*īśā*) and of Brahma when he was viewed as the highest God, virtually co-existent with *brahman*. Later, sectarian followers of Viṣṇu and Śiva applied it also to their chosen god when making the point that, besides being the highest God and chief among the three gods of Trimūrti, he was also the actual transcendent Absolute or *brahman*. The term came to be used even for the Buddha in post-canonical literature (Milindapañha, Visuddhimagga), perhaps in the sense of 'self-dependent'. Later it was taken up by Mahāyāna Buddhism in the original sense and applied to the Ādi Buddha (cf. the complex stūpa outside Kathmandu known as Svayambhunath, i.e. the self-existent Lord).

***svayaṁvara*** (vern. *svayaṁbara*, 'own choice') an ancient Indo-Āryan ceremony or betrothal festival, often in the form of a contest or tournament, at which daughters of royal and other noble families chose their husbands. It is of IE antiquity as transpires from European folk stories and fairy-tales.

**Symbol** (*cihna*) a representation of a transcendent, otherwise inaccessible, abstract or absent reality. Symbols play a most important part in Hinduism: in ritual, worship, scriptural sources and meditational procedures.

***śabda*** sound; message; evidence; testimony; manifested truth; revelation; truth expressed in the scriptural sources; revealed scripture, i.e. the Veda.

**Śaiva, Śaivite** pertaining to god Śiva; Śivaistic.

**Śaiva Siddhānta** a sectarian movement which grew out of the mystic and devotional poetry of Nāyaṉmārs. Originating in the twelfth century A.D. or before, it is a kind of parallel development to the Vaiṣṇava *bhakti* movement. It stresses Śiva's grace, mediated to the follower by his *guru*, through whom he attains intimate union with Śiva. Its canon is *Tirumurai*, the anthology of hymns of 63 Nāyaṉmārs, arranged in eleven books.

**Śakas** (Scythians) an IE people (known also from ancient Gr. sources) who, displaced from Central Asia by Tocharians, settled for a time in Afghanistan around the turn of the era and also ruled North Western India. They subsequently participated with Parthians in the wider conquest of North India.

**Śakra** ('strong') an epithet of Indra, sometimes used as his name (especially in Pl. texts as Sakka).

**Śākta** related to the *śakti* cult; a sectarian follower and worshipper of the Goddess or Śakti Devī.

***śakti*** power, potency; divine creative force; usually regarded as female in character, it often appears in personalized form as the consort of a god, and sometimes as the Goddess in her own right. The cult of *śakti* is of ancient origin and its traces can be found also in the Vedas: in the references to goddesses-wives of gods, in the so-called Devī Sūkta (RV 10,125), in the role of the female element symbolized by cosmic waters in creation myths etc. It eventually expressed itself strongly in Tantric teachings and practices.

***śālagrāma*** a black ammonite stone containing fossilized shells of an extinct species of mollusc, found in the Gaṇḍakī river near a village called Śālagrāma (i.e. 'village of śāla trees', *Vatica robusta*). It is sacred to Viṣṇu and highly prized by his followers.

***śaṅkara*** auspicious; an epithet of Śiva.

**Śaṅkara** (788–820) the greatest writer of the Advaita Vedānta school of thought, which he arguably made into the most influential of the six orthodox *darṣaṇas* of Hinduism. He expounded it in his commentaries to the Upaniṣads, BS and the BhG. Some other works are attributed to him, including devotional poems in Sanskrit of which many are still used in worship as devotional songs (*bhajans*). During his lifetime, which would appear short (but the first date may refer to the year of his renunciation), he travelled widely, engaged in disputations with opponents, and taught his philosophy also at royal courts. He is reputed to have founded the Daśanāmī Order of *saṁnyāsis* which still exists and has four monastic centres of learning whose heads hold the title of Śaṅkarācāryas.

***śānti*** peace, tranquillity; often used at the end of religious treatises as an invocation; a ritual for preventing disease.

***śarīra*** (physical) body; bodily relics after cremation.

***śāsana*** a discipline; a set of rules; a teaching tradition.

***śāstra*** rule, treatise, textbook; post-Vedic compilatory works on traditional knowledge, especially with respect to social life, customs and laws.

**Śatapatha Brāhmaṇa** the longest and most important priestly book which belongs to VS of the YV.

***śauca*** purity; cleansing oneself from defilements; uprightness, honesty; one of the *niyamas* in Patañjali's *aṣṭaṅga yoga.*

**Śeṣa** ('remainder') the cosmic serpent, called also Ananta and symbolizing eternity, or suspended time, on whom Viṣṇu-Nārāyaṇa sleeps during the cosmic night between the last dissolution of the universe and its new manifestation. His coils are supposed to represent the endlessly repetitive cycles of time.

***śikhara*** temple tower erected over the inner sanctuary containing the effigy of the god.

***śiśna*** the male organ of generation.

**Śiśnadeva** the deity of the erect male organ.

***śiṣya*** pupil, disciple; scholar.

***śiva*** auspicious, gracious; a propitiatory epithet of the Vedic god Rudra, (cf. RV 2,33), who probably merged with a powerful indigenous deity (the 'proto-Śiva' of Harappan civilization) and other influences, including tribal ones, to become the complex god Śiva.

**Śiva** the Lord of creatures and of the creative cosmic power symbolized by the *liṅga*, and of the spiritual mastery of reality epitomized by yoga. His *liṅga* is also representative of the cosmic pillar, the *axis mundi*. In Brahminic theology he is the third member of the divine Trinity (Trimūrti) as God Destroyer represented by his form as Naṭarāja. His sectarian followers regard him as identical with the transcendent *brahman* as well as being the highest God and ruler of creation. His wife and *śakti* was originally Umā, but she has many forms or incarnations, the most frequent one being Pārvatī who appears with him in many mythological stories. His weapon and emblem is the trident (*triśūla*) and his vehicle is Nandi, the bull, both well-known from medieval icons and first seen with him on Kuṣāna coins. In Purāṇic mythology, which is foreshadowed also in the Vedas, he alone was immortal among the gods before *amṛta* was obtained by them and he, therefore, could drink the poison produced during the churning of the cosmic ocean and rescue the other gods and the world, a feat which caused his throat to become blue.

**Śivānanda** (1887–1963) originally a medical doctor, he became a wandering yogi at the age of 40 and founded an *āśram* in 1932 in Rishikesh. He wrote numerous popular treatises on the practice of yoga and on Hindu religious philosophy and had pupils round the world. He succeeded particularly in propagating a mild form of Hatha Yoga practice. His Divine Life Society, founded in 1936, reached its peak in the sixties and seventies, but has declined somewhat since then.

**Śivarātri** (Śiva's night) is every fourteenth night of the dark half of every lunar month. His great night, Mahāśivarātri, is in the lunar month of Māgha (January/February), or in some parts of India in Phālguna (February/March) and it is celebrated by all castes with elaborate rituals and offerings to *liṅga* images in memory of the event when Śiva revealed himself to Brahma and Viṣṇu in the form of a flaming column (*jyotirliṅga*).

**Śiva Saṁhitā** a late Sanskrit work (possibly seventeenth or eighteenth century) on Hatha Yoga and its philosophical and Tantric context.

***śloka*** a verse in the epic metre consisting of two lines of sixteen syllables each.

***śraddhā*** faith; often regarded as essential towards one's *guru*, faith is sometimes interpreted in a milder way as confidence in the truth and efficacy of spiritual teachings which is a necessary prerequisite for starting a spiritual practice through which one's confidence can eventually be verified by one's own experience.

***śrāddha*** a supplementary rite to the funerary ceremony; *pūjā* to ancestors consisting of water and cakes (*piṇḍa*) intended to feed their ethereal bodies in the afterlife, thus averting or postponing their repeated death.

***śramaṇa*** ascetic; renunciate; homeless wanderer seeking spiritual fulfilment. The movement of *śramaṇas* reached its peak in the time of the early Upaniṣads when most of them were 'dropouts' from the Vedic-Brahminic tradition, by then spiritually sterile, or successors of unorthodox early wanderers such as *keśins* or Vrātyas. There were among them individuals practising extreme austerities of most varied kinds, philosophical thinkers, yogis and meditators as well as precursors of Tantric practices. From this background emerged both Buddhism and Jainism.

**Śrauta Sūtra** a writing elucidating some part of *śruti*.

***śreṇi*** occupational guild. Guilds may already have existed in Vedic times, but were recorded from the fifth century B.C. onwards.

**Śrī** (lustre) goddess of beauty and good fortune who emerged from the churning of the cosmic ocean, later identified with

Lakṣmī; an honorific prefixed to names of gods and names of prominent persons.

***śruti*** that which was heard, i.e. revealed; revelation; the summary designation of scriptures which have the status of divine revelation in Hinduism, i.e. the four Vedas, the Brāhmaṇas, Āraṇyakas and Upaniṣads.

**Śuddha Śaiva** a sect with its own 28 *āgamas* which it regards as 'pure' because directly revealed by Śiva, and hence as a divine revelation. Besides ritual, it employs yoga to achieve salvation in union with Śiva.

***śūdra*** servant, labourer; member of the lowest (subservient) of the four main Hindu castes. To begin with it consisted of the conquered original inhabitants of North India and of prisoners of war. In later centuries the barrier between them and *vaiśyas* broke down as a result of occupational overlaps and changing family fortunes so that nowadays it is difficult to distinguish one from the other.

**Śuṅga** a North Indian dynasty (183–73 B.C.) which succeeded the Mauryas and was instrumental in the revival of Brāhmanism and thereby in the formation of what was to become Hinduism.

***śūnya*** empty, void; empty space (*ākāśa*); zero; zero symbolizing *brahman* or *nirvāṇa*.

***śūnyatā*** emptiness, voidness; metaphysical voidness of things as unsubstantial or devoid of their own essence. This is in the first place a Mahāyāna Buddhist term, expressing the idea that things and beings, and indeed all reality, are devoid of any conceptually graspable essence. In the Tantric context, however, it came to be associated with the symbol of *yoni*, which suggests the idea of a hidden germ within so that *śūnyatā* came to mean a 'potent' void, and since Tantrism frequently possesses both Buddhist and Hindu connotations, this potent void came to be seen as harbouring both the seed of enlightenment and the seeds of manifestation.

***śvetāmbara*** (white-clad) the name of the sect of Jain mendicants who abandoned the earlier tradition of going about naked (still continued by *digambaras*) and adopted a white garment.

**Ṣaṣṭhī, Ṣaṣṭhījāgara** a folk goddess regarded as a form of Durgā, presiding over the sixth day after the birth of a child. Her mount is a cat.

**Tagore** (Thākur) a prominent Bengali family whose several members contributed substantially to the Hindu reform movement. Chief among them were Devendranāth (1818–1905), a religious reformer who was active in Brāhmo Samāj affairs, later turning to mysticism and settling in his retreat in Śāntiniketan; and his son Rabindranāth (1861–1941), poet and writer, who won the Nobel Prize for literature in 1913. Greatly influenced by the Upaniṣads, some Buddhist texts, and the Bāul path as well as European poets such as Shelley and Wordsworth, Rabindranāth expressed his main spiritual vision in his work *Sādhanā*. In 1921 he founded the Viśva Bhāratī World University in Śāntiniketan which attracted many prominent teachers and had among its pupils some who, in their later lives, played substantial roles in Indian cultural and public life. It is still a significant educational institution in present-day India.

***tamas*** darkness; inertia; one of the three *guṇas* (dynamic forces) of *prakṛti*, the other two being *sattva* (purity) and *rajas* (energy).

***tāṇḍava*** Śiva's cosmic dance as the symbol of the divine play (*līlā*), repeatedly manifesting itself as the creation, duration and destruction of the universe.

***tantra*** thread, threads in a loom; web; metaphorically: guideline through the labyrinth of *saṁsāra* towards liberation.

**Tantras** textual sources or *āgamas* of Tantrism which started appearing around the seventh century A.D.

**Tantric cult** is oriented towards the evocation of the divine creative energy or *śakti* represented by spouses of the gods and concentrated in the idea and the various forms of the Goddess or Devī. Its essential ingredients are: elaborate symbolical ritual which involves all the senses, great use of *mudrās* and *mantras*, visualization of *mūrtis* and construction and use of *maṇḍalas* for ritual and meditational purposes. Left-handed Tantric practice goes beyond symbolism in involving the senses and incorporates direct sensory experiences into its ritual of the five M's (*pañcamākāra*), i.e. partaking in the communion consisting of *mada*, *māṁsa*, *matsya*, *mudrā* and *maithuna* and accompanied by elaborate rituals. It is seldom stressed in modern writings on the subject, but it is important to bear in mind that, ideally, the rituals and all the procedures should be performed in a state of meditational exaltation.

**Tantric Yoga** a spiritual path which aims at reaching the ultimate experience of transcendental unity by integrating the opposites, manifested in the world especially in sexual polarity. The integration of opposites on all levels is therefore seen as the most effective means of progress. The Tantric Yoga practice has four stages: (1) Kriyā Yoga involves public rituals, *japa* on special *mantras* called *dhāraṇīs*, and scriptural study; (2) Caryā Yoga prescribes the observance of virtues, further and deeper study, meditation and, after initiation, the regular performance of esoteric rituals which symbolize the path to enlightenment; (3) Mahā Yoga is a technique of the 'interiorization' of the ritual achieved by visualizational techniques; and finally (4) Anuttarā Yoga is supposed to lead to the achievement of final integration through, in the right-handed practice (*dakṣinācāra*), the process of meditational identification of the *sādhaka* with the chosen god, who is visualized in union with his *śakti*, and in the left-handed practice (*vāmācāra*) through assumption by the *sādhaka* and his *dākiṇī* themselves of the *maithuna* position in which they represent, and in their minds 'become', the god and his *śakti*. This is supposed to enhance their meditational achievement of the final integration and their liberation in the samādhic experience of *mahāsukha*. It will be obvious that to reach the stage of Anuttarā Yoga in one's practice, whether right-handed or left-handed, with a realistic chance of progress, presupposes mastery of the previous stages which will have taken years of dedicated practice.

**Tantrism** a school of spiritual teachings and practices, both Hindu and Buddhist, stressing the necessity of involving all the constituents and dynamic forces of the human personality, including the emotions and bodily functions, in the process of spiritual endeavour, and recognizing their affinity and interrelatedness with the cosmic forces and the need to integrate them consciously into the global scheme of universal reality. This involves recognition of the existence of polarity and its purposeful, practical incorporation into both the Tantric cult and the Tantric spiritual path on all existential levels in order to achieve final integration and thereby the goal of ultimate fulfilment and liberation. Tantrism has its roots in the ancient traditions of the Harappan civilization, in some Vedic creation myths and rituals, in ancient IE folk festivals which survived as a substream even during the time of prevalence of the high Vedic and Brahminic cults, in certain Vrātya practices which are to some extent reflected in the AV, and also in some tribal customs which were absorbed into Hinduism. It came to prominence in Gupta times, but subsided during the Islamic period and has always been shrouded in secrecy, which also undoubtedly made misuse easier. The Tantric sources often claim that Tantrism represents the school of thought and practice, both ritual and spiritual, best suited for the present Kali Yuga age. Much is still to be done in the line of research into Tantric sources and their elucidation.

***tapas*** as m.: an epithet of Agni; as n.: heat; inner flame, creative power, spiritual energy; observance of a spiritual discipline; penance; austerity; ascetic practice; meditational drive; one of the *niyamas* in Patañjali's *aṣṭaṅga yoga*. In the creation myths of the Brāhmaṇas we learn that the demiurge or the Creator god first generates *tapas* in himself by inner exertion and follows this by bringing forth manifestation and fashioning the world. *Tapas* therefore appears to mean a spiritual creative power of a neutral kind available from the inner resources of the individual god. There is no suggestion of a duality or of an inner tension derived from an intrinsic polarity as is the case with the gods later so prominent in Hinduism, whose creative energy is expressed in terms of a feminine counterpart to their masculinity, which is called *śakti* (f.) and outwardly appears as their spouse. Both these trends appear to be equally ancient in origin and are reflected in differing approaches to the spiritual path, one stressing renunciation and a strict external and mental discipline (e.g. the *śramaṇa* movement, early Buddhism and Jainism, Patañjali's Yoga system, Vedāntic Jñāna, Ramaṇa of Arunachala) and the other advocating a global approach and the integration of polarities, and incorporating active life into the spiritual discipline (e.g. part of the Vrātya movement, some types of Kriyā Yoga, Bāuls, Bhakti Mārga, Mahāyāna Buddhism, Buddhist and Hindu Tantrism, Aurobindo).

**Tārā** ('star'), also: Tārakā a goddess who is, according to Purāṇic mythology, the wife of Bṛhaspati. She was temporarily abducted by Soma, the Moon god, and as a result gave birth to Budha, the Wise one, which is also the name of the planet Mercury. In Tantrism Tārā appears to be the esoteric form of Devī. It is possible that she was an ancient non-Vedic goddess, associated with the cult of the Great Mother. She also plays a prominent role in Vajrayāna Buddhism under several guises, particularly as the White Tārā and the Green Tārā.

***tattva*** truth; reality; true nature; true state; first principle; element; primary substance (evolved from *prakṛti*); later also: level of reality.

***tat tvam asi*** 'thou art that' (CU 6,8,7; 6,9,4; 6,14,3), one of the four 'Great Sayings' (*mahāvākyas*) of the Upaniṣads expressing the Vedāntic philosophy of oneness, widely popularized as a basic Hindu tenet about the divine essence present deep down in everything and everybody.

***tejas*** light, brilliance; vital power; fiery energy; glory; splendour; majesty.

**Temple (*mandira*)** the house of god used for worship and ritual offerings. In Vedic and Brāhmanic times, altars for worship and ritual sacrifices were constructed in the open. New ones were built for each occasion. Shrines for popular worship were mostly under sacred trees and in natural caves. Hindu temples developed in emulation of rock-carved Buddhist assembly halls for monks living in their cells in monastic communities. The assembly halls had a stūpa opposite the entrance, indicating the Buddha's presence, later supplemented or replaced by a statue of the preaching Buddha to whom simple *pūjās* were offered by monks and visiting lay people. Originally, the Buddhist assembly halls were of light wooden construction, as they developed from summer pavilions in gardens where the Buddha and his monks used to spend the rainy seasons and which were often donated to him or to the Order of monks for permanent use. Consequently the assembly halls were afterwards built of brick for greater durability and from the second century B.C. were also carved into rocks where a community of monks would adopt natural caves for their abodes. (This eventually led to whole complexes of Buddhist cells and halls being carved in rocks, such as Karli or Ajantā.) The first Hindu rock-carved places of worship are known from cca 400 A.D. Simple stone structures soon followed in places where no rocks were available and the full-scale Hindu temples emerged around A.D. 600. A Hindu temple consists of the main hall (*maṇḍapa*), the main shrine with a *mūrti* in the sacred cell called the 'womb-house (*garbhagṛha*), which has a tower (*śikhara*) over it, and a number of subsidiary halls (*mandiras*) and shrines with further *mūrtis*, walled courtyards and gates (in South India with tall towers over them called *gopuras*). Outside the main hall is always a flagpole (*dhvaja*), a reminder of the Vedic sacrificial pole (*yūpa*) and a symbol of the world axis.

***ṭhag*** (vern.; fr. Skt. verbal root *sthag*, 'to conceal') member of a secret sect of devotees of Kālī in the form of Bhavānī (she still has a temple in Mirzāpur, near Varāṇasī) who worshipped her by bringing her human sacrifices, which they usually obtained by the strangulation of unsuspecting victims. The earliest references to the existence of the sect date from the seventh century A.D. It was suppressed under the British Governor-General Lord Bentinck in a comprehensive campaign in 1831–7, but small groups were still being hunted till 1861. Individual instances of the practice occurred even after that and the last recorded execution of an offender took place in 1882 in Pañjāb. There was a parallel Muslim movement of Fidā'sīs (devoted ones), a branch of the Shī-ite sect, known as Hurs in India. The Hindu and Muslim groups often mingled. There is little doubt that purely criminal elements from both the Hindu and Muslim communities also joined the movement to achieve 'higher' status within the criminal world and for the opportunity it offered them to carry out robberies. (The word entered English vocabulary in the anglicized form 'thug', meaning 'cut-throat, ruffian, violent criminal'.)

***ṭhagī*** the practice of religious strangulation of a human victim as an offering to goddess Kālī. (The anglicized form 'thuggee' is sometimes used in the original sense of *ṭhag*, i.e. member of the sect of stranglers, to distinguish them from the 'thugs' of modern society.)

**Theosophical Society** an organization founded in New York in 1875 by Mrs. H. P. Blavatksy, who was of Russian origin, and Colonel H. S. Olcott, with the object of promoting universal brotherhood of humanity and the study of comparative religion and philosophy, and above all to engage in practical exploration of the mystic or occult aspects of life and reality. In 1879 its headquarters were moved to India as the home of ancient wisdom and established in Adyār near Madrās. Its syncretic teachings contain many tenets of Hinduism, particularly the doctrine of rebirth or reincarnation and of final liberation, but it also incorporates the purely European concept of evolution presented as an ideal of steady progress towards the final spiritual goal of perfection, on the part both of the individual and of mankind as a whole, thus representing a kind of spiritual darwinism. Its founders and most subsequent representatives supported Indian endeavours to gain political independence and the Society was instrumental in encouraging the self-confidence of Hindus in the face of strong activities by Christian missions, and it helped greatly in improving the standing of Hinduism among world religions. It has been and still is important for Hindu studies, even on the academic level, by maintaining a vast collection of religious manuscripts and promoting research into Hindu religious sources and the publication of its results.

**Tilak, Bal Gangadhar** (1857–1920) a nationalistic politician and a Hindu revivalist with Vedāntic leanings who stressed the antiquity of Hinduism, wrote a commentary on the BhG and promoted Hindu festivals, all in the cause of awakening Hindus to national self-awareness and to political action for freedom.

***tilaka*** a sectarian mark on the forehead of a follower. It is likely to have developed from the traditional sacred mark made on the forehead, symbolizing the third eye (the eye of wisdom, see *bindu*). There are many elaborate marks used by sectarian *sādhus*, but generally those containing vertical lines indicate Viṣṇuite and those with horizontal lines Śaivite allegiance. The rarely seen marks containing a triangle and a circle might once have indicated an allegiance to Brahma, but would nowadays mean acceptance by the bearer of the whole Trimūrti. Śākta sects use the *svastika*.

**Time** (*kāla*) recognized in the Vedas as a primordial power or even the 'first principle' of manifestation, it is understood in Purāṇic as well as philosophical Hinduism as a relative component of manifested reality experienced at a different pace by different categories of beings, while the Supreme God or the ultimate reality and those who reached it are regarded as being beyond time.

***tīrtha*** passage, road, ford; place for crossing over from this world to the nether world or to the dimension of liberation; a place of pilgrimage, especially if it is believed that a pilgrim who dies there goes straight to heaven or is liberated.

***tīrthaṁkara*** (ford-maker) a designation used mainly in Jainism for the succession of Jain enlightened teachers, although it may occur also in a Hindu context. The last (historical) one was Vardhamāna Mahāvīra, a contemporary of the Buddha.

***torana*** gateway.

**Transmigration** of individuals from life to life, known from ancient Greece as *metempsychosis*, is the basis of the Hindu view of life in virtually all schools of thought and sects and it is combined with the teaching of retribution for one's deeds according to the principle 'as you have sown, so you will reap' which is believed to have the force of a natural law. The beginning of the sequence of successive lives cannot be envisaged, since its course is understood not as proceeding along a linear flow of time, but as moving in never-ending circles (see *saṁsāra*). But although its beginning cannot be ascertained, it can be stopped or escaped by the individual, if he takes a conscious decision to achieve liberation or salvation and persists in working it out for himself as described in various traditional and sectarian teachings and systems of spiritual practice.

***trayī vidyā*** the threefold knowledge of the brahmins; Vedic hymns, sacrificial procedures and chanting of *mantras*.

***tretā*** triad; a throw of dice showing three dots.

**Tretā Yuga** the second age of the Purāṅic history of the world, lasting 1,296,000 years. It corresponds to the legendary Silver age of Greek mythology.

**Trika, Trikaśāsana** a Kashmiri Śaiva system of philosophy which reached its peak with Vasugupta (770–830 A.D.) who is sometimes credited with its foundation. However, it did have some prehistory, and it flourished for several hundred years after him. It is, at bottom, monistic in the Advaitic vein, but contains some Sāṅkhya elements. It recognizes three ultimate principles: (1) Śiva as the all-knowing and all-sustaining being or *ātman*, (2) *śakti* as his transcendental energy, and (3) *aṇu*, the individual *ātman*, which is in essence identical with Śiva, but is caught in *saṁsāra* as a result of *māyā* and the activities of Śiva's *śakti*. Salvation can be brought about if the individual sees through the veil of *māyā* and discovers his identity with Śiva. This can be accomplished by the adoption of the devotional path (*bhaktimārga*) into which one has to be initiated by a *guru*. Finding the right *guru* is the result of Śiva's grace, which is also needed to reach the final union with him.

***trikoṇa*** a triangle; vulva.

***trikoṇa yantra*** a *yantra* diagram of two intersected triangles in which the downward-pointing one represents the male principle or God and the upward-pointing one the female principle or *śakti*. There are also more complicated *yantras* comprising multiple triangles with complex symbolism used in yoga and in Tantric rituals and meditation.

**Trimūrti** the Hindu trinity of gods, viz. Brahma the Creator, Viṣṇu the Preserver and Śiva the Destroyer, which is interpreted as symbolizing the everlasting flow of the ever-recurring manifestations of reality in its three aspects of the creation, duration and destruction of the universe. This is reflected also in the successive lives of all individual beings as their birth, a span of existence and death, and indeed in all other phenomena of reality which have their beginning and a period of duration, followed by inevitable decay and disintegration only to be recycled in the never-ending process of becoming. The first indication of a trinity of gods can be found in the Maitrī Upaniṣad (4,5) which mentions Brahma, Rudra and Viṣṇu along with other deities and various phenomena as subjects of meditation and proclaims them to be forms of *brahman* (4,6). Next (5,1–2) the Upaniṣad names Brahma, Viṣṇu and Rudra with Prajāpati, Agni, Varuṇa, Vāyu, Indra and a few other, lesser, deities and forces and proclaims them to be identical with the tranquil and hidden self (*ātman*). This self is nevertheless the lord and maker of all and appears in that capacity as Prajāpati, whose essence is immeasurable consciousness or intelligence (*cetāmātra*), but he has further characteristics which lead him to create the multiplicity of the world, namely *rajas*, *sattva* and *tamas* (later known as the *guṇas* of *prakṛti*). These are manifested as his agents Brahma, Viṣṇu and Rudra. The correlation which the Upaniṣad makes between the three *guṇas* and the three gods accurately reflects their later epithets of Creator, Preserver and Destroyer. The actual elaboration of the trinity teaching appears to have been a product of the theological speculations of brahmins, seeking to create an 'umbrella' system during the time of Brahminic revival amidst the proliferation of many divisive sectarian movements and the emergence of a profusion of local deities. It is incorporated mainly in the Purāṇic sources, but despite all the effort of the theologians it has never gained great popularity, being overshadowed by the cults of individual gods, mainly Viṣṇu and Śiva. In their mythologies the trinity continues a kind of shadowy existence in that the sectarian sources undertake to demonstrate the superiority of their respective god over the other two. Other popular cults are centred around the figure of Kṛṣṇa, the various forms of the Goddess and latterly also Gaṇeśa.

**Tripura** ('triple city') the name of the mythical city of *asuras*, built of gold, silver and iron.

***triṣūla*** trident; three-pronged spear, the emblem and weapon of some deities, particularly of Śiva. For his sectarian followers, who regard him as the sole divinity, it incorporates the whole Trinity. For those Śaiva followers who practise Kuṇḍalinī Yoga it further symbolically represents the three main *nāḍīs*: *suṣumnā*, *iḍā* and *piṅgalā*. It is also carried by sectarian *sādhus*.

**Trita Āptya** an obscure Vedic deity who sometimes appears to have served as a scapegoat, because it was believed that guilt could be transferred onto him.

**Trivikrama** an epithet of Viṣṇu referring to his feat of the three great strides by which he gained rulership of the universe in the form of Vāmana, the dwarf incarnation.

**Truth** is understood in all Hindu thought either explicitly or implicitly as having two levels. What appears true in everyday life or on the phenomenal level may not be true on the absolute or noumenal level. The absolute truth if expressed in relative terms of speech cannot lead to adequate understanding, but it may be a guideline on the path to the direct apprehension of absolute truth. The boundary between the two levels of truth often appears to be flexible and seems to shift from school to school, but all schools do agree that in the last instance the absolute truth has to be experienced directly, rather than transmitted conceptually, metaphorically, symbolically or by any other means, although such limited means are necessary and useful initial devices to arouse interest and encourage practical steps for the purpose of developing the capability to experience truth directly.

**Tulsīdās** (sixteenth century, possibly 1543–1623) the seventh in succession as the leader and teacher of Rāmānanda's *bhakti* movement. He was the author of a highly influential poetical work in Hindi based on the Rāmāyaṇa, called *Rāmacaritamānasa* (The Lake of Rāma's Deeds).

***turīya*** (also: *caturtha*) the 'fourth state', a term used in some Upaniṣads and Vedāntic works for the accomplished state of consciousness in which the final truth or the experience of one's identity with the ultimate reality is fully and consciously realized.

The other three states are: waking state, dream state and deep sleep state, the last one being regarded as a temporary unconscious unification with the ultimate reality.

**Tvaṣṭar** the divine artisan; fashioner of the universe, acting as the demiurge during the process of creation. He is also responsible for giving to all living beings their particular forms. In order to carry out this task he oversees their gestation period in the womb.

***udgātar*** the priest whose task is the chanting of the hymns of the SV during the Vedic ritual.

***udumbara*** a sacred tree, *Ficus glomerata*, from whose wood are made sacrificial posts and other implements.

**Ugratārā** (*ugra*=mighty, terrible) the wrathful form of the Tantric goddess Tārā.

**Ujjayinī** (Ujjain) one of the sacred cities of Hinduism, its early name being Avanti. One of the four places where according to legend fell some drops of *amṛta*, the drink of immortality, when the gods and demons fought over it. This is commemorated by a Kuṁbha Mela every twelve years. The other three places are: Haridvāra (Hardwār), Nāsik and Prayāga.

**Ultimate Reality** the highest concept of religion or of religious philosophy which is perhaps best expressed in mainstream Hinduism by the Upaniṣadic twin term *brahman/ātman* denoting the impersonal or suprapersonal spiritual essence and source of all that is (of reality as a whole) which is at the same time the essence or the self of every individual being. It therefore also includes the feature of personhood, although infinitely elevated above the limitations of a human personality. (This is sometimes expressed in theological language by the concept of 'the infinite personality of God'.) Individual schools and sects within Hinduism use a variety of terms, sometimes preferring one which leans more towards the personal aspect and designates the Ultimate Reality as the Supreme Lord or refers to the Ultimate by a chosen name, such as Viṣṇu or Śiva, or Devī, the Goddess, because of the need of their followers to form a personal bond. All this basically indicates that the nature of the one Ultimate does not fit into any neat conceptual framework, but combines seemingly contradictory modes of being within itself. This, however, is precisely why approaches to the Ultimate from different vantage-points, according to the initial position of the truth-seeker, are possible.

**Umā** ('light') an early name of the Goddess; the reborn Satī, wife of Rudra/Śiva, who more often appears as such under her name of Pārvatī, the daughter of Himavat.

**Untouchables** outcasts; those whose mere touch pollutes a caste Hindu; in the official language of India today: 'scheduled classes'. They are descendants of groups which were not incorporated into the caste system. Among them were some sections of the conquered pre-Āryan inhabitants, some primitive tribal communities and even Āryans who for some reason lost their caste. They had to live on the fringe of the Āryan settlements, performing for them tasks regarded as low or unclean, e.g. as refuse collectors, carriers of corpses, executioners of criminals, hunters, fishermen, leather workers etc. In imitation of the Āryan caste divisions the untouchables themselves developed internal caste barriers, and even had their own outcasts. Many restrictions were placed on them when they entered an Āryan settlement and they were denied access to Hindu temples. Some modern reform movements have tried to alleviate their lot, but their greatest champion was Gāndhī, who called them Harijans (children of God). Independent India outlawed untouchability and special measures have been introduced to enable the scheduled classes to have access to education and higher occupations, a task still hampered by social prejudice and the hostility of Brahminic extremists. In order to escape their stigma, a large number of untouchables in India embraced Buddhism, following the public conversion of their leader Dr. Ambedkar in 1956, but to little avail.

***upādhi*** attribute, mark; limitation, condition; disguise; a term applied in Advaitic thought to explain the difference between *brahman* as the sole absolute reality and the illusory multiple phenomenal reality superimposed on *brahman* by the ignorant mind, as when it mistakenly superimposes the notion of 'snake' on a rope seen in semi-darkness.

***upanayana*** the initiation ceremony of a boy into his caste, called the second birth, at which he receives his sacred cord worn across the left shoulder under his garments. This ceremony takes place between the age of eight and eleven, according to caste, and it does not apply to *śūdras* who, consequently, are not called twice-born.

**Upaniṣads** philosophical and mystical writings included in the *śruti* part of Vedic literature as its 'end' or closing part (hence called summarily also Vedānta). Believed to be divinely inspired, they are accepted as having scriptural authority in Hinduism, but there is no full agreement about their number. The following thirteen oldest Upaniṣads can be regarded as Vedic: Bṛhadāraṇyaka, Chāndogya, Aitareya, Taittirīya, Īśa, Kena, Kaṭha, Praśna, Muṇḍaka, Māṇḍūkya, Śvetāśvatara, Kauṣītakī and Maitrī. Some Hindu authorities, however, accept 108 Upaniṣads as authentic *śruti*. Many more treatises exist which use the term Upaniṣad in their title, some written even in modern times. The main message of the Upaniṣads can be summarized in four points: (1) The deepest essence of all reality called *brahman*, which is also the divine source of the universe, is identical with the innermost self of man (*ātman*). (2) As long as one does not realize it, one is subject to a seemingly endless round of rebirths in various forms of existence according to karmic merit. (3) A conscious realisation of the essential identity of one's innermost self and the divine source of reality leads to liberation (*mokṣa*). (4) The way to this realisation involves detachment from worldly concerns and the development of direct inner knowledge through techniques of meditation (*dhyāna*), later developed into a systematic discipline known as *yoga*.

***upāsanā*** service, attendance, engagement, worship, adoration; reflection, spiritual meditation.

**Upavedas** auxiliary branches of learning attached to the Vedic tradition. They contain elements of great antiquity, but were composed in post-Vedic centuries. They are: Āyurveda (on medicine), Dhanurveda (on archery), Gandharvaveda (on music) and Śilpa Śāstra (on architecture and sculpture).

***urṇā*** a mark or a circle of hair between the eyebrows; a symbol of the third eye (of wisdom or enlightenment) depicted on effigies of some gods, but mostly on the statues of the Buddha and *bodhisattvas*. Cf. *bindu*.

**Urvaśī** an *apsaras* of extreme beauty, the only one of her kind ever to be referred to by name in the RV. Her story is told in the SB, the Mhb and the Purāṇas. She charmed even the gods Mitra and Varuṇa, in some unusual manner conceiving and then giving birth to their sons Agastya and Vasiṣṭha, but the incident displeased them and she was banned from heaven. She then lived on earth quite happily with prince Pururavas, but was tricked by the *gandharvas*, who missed her charms, to return to heaven, the ban having been apparently lifted. Purūravas desperately searched for her and when she bore him a son from their union, she arranged to meet him several more times, giving birth to more sons by him. As he never tired of hardships in search of her when she was not with him, he was eventually granted residence in heaven after fulfilling certain conditions. The story was used by Kālidāsa in his drama *Vikramorvaśī* ('The Hero and the Nymph').

**Uṣas** the goddess of dawn (cf. Aurora) who opens the gate in the morning for the chariot of Sūrya, the Sun god. Great admiration of her was expressed in a number of hymns of praise in the RV in verses of outstanding lyrical beauty.

***uṣṇīṣa*** turban, head-band, coronet; a protuberance on the top of the head of effigies of accomplished saints (corresponding to the *sahasrāra padma* of Kuṇḍalinī Yoga) and of the Buddha.

***uttara*** upper, higher, superior; northern; future, posterior.

**Uttara Mīmāṁsā** the orthodox name of the Vedāntic system of philosophy, one of the six Hindu *darṣaṇas*. See Advaita, Viṣiṣṭa Advaita and Dvaita.

***vāc, vāk*** speech; in the Vedas it is a cosmic divine force (comparable to the Biblical Logos).

**Vāc, Vāk** goddess of speech, the 'mother of the Vedas'.

***vāhana*** vehicle, conveyance, carrier; mount, an animal used for riding on. Virtually every higher deity of the Hindu Pantheon has a carrier or mount from the animal kingdom, sometimes of a mythical character, e.g. Brahma the goose or swan, Śiva the bull, Ganeṣa the rat or mouse, Varuṇa the fish or the *makara* (a crocodile-like sea monster), Viṣṇu the mythical bird-like creature Garuḍa etc.

**Vaikunṭha** the name of Viṣṇu's paradise.

***vairāgya*** the overcoming of passion; passionlessness. It is an achievement which is a condition of progress in Jñāna Yoga.

**Vaiśālī** (Pl. Vesālī) an ancient city north of Patna which was the capital of a kingdom in Buddha's time.

**Vaiśeṣika** one of the six systems of Hindu thought, a kind of natural philosophy, expounding the atomic theory and classifying reality into six categories: substance, quality, action, universality, particularity and inherence.

**Vaiṣṇava, Vaiṣṇavite** pertaining to god Viṣṇu, Viṣṇuistic.

***vaiśya*** member of the third (professional) of the four main Hindu castes.

***vajra*** thunderbolt; the weapon of Indra and Kārttiyeya; diamond; symbol of enlightenment.

**Vajrayāna** the 'diamond' vehicle or Tantric school of Buddhism, predominantly right-handed, although left-hand practices also occurred, especially in mixed Hindu-Buddhist context.

**Vallabha** (1479–1531) the founder of a Vaiṣṇava sect in Gujarāt in the wake of his two visions of Kṛṣṇa while on pilgrimages to Vṛndāvana. He is believed by his followers to have been Kṛṣṇa's incarnation. He wrote commentaries on BS and BP and taught 'pure non-duality' (*śuddhādvaita*) or identity of the world and selves with Kṛṣṇa. This fact is obscured in individuals by ignorance created by *māyā* in the process of manifestation, but is restored by Kṛṣṇa's grace if one abandons oneself in continuous worship of him by following ritually the pattern of his life in one or all of four possible roles: as Kṛṣṇa's servant, companion, parent or lover. The first three forms of worship consist of ritual care for Kṛṣṇa's effigy accompanied by music, singing and sometimes dancing, and the last one involves role-playing as a *gopī* (a virtual psychological and behavioural sex change which, however, remains confined to the context of worship, even if it is of longer duration as during festivals or on pilgrimage, and does not involve change in one's role in real life). Like Kṛṣṇa, Vallabha got married, and the leadership of the sect has been passed on through sons. This eventually led to the forming of subsects whose leaders adopted the title of Mahārājas (cf. one 'Guru Mahārāj Ji' who arrived in the West in the 1980s). At times the emphasis on the literal re-enactment in communal ritual of Kṛṣṇa's dalliance (*līlā*) with the *gopīs* led to abuses. One such instance was exposed in a court case in Bombay in 1862, but the sect survived this and other scandals and still functions.

**Vālmīki** a legendary hermit reputed to have been the author of the Rāmāyaṇa who is himself represented in it as taking part in the story.

**Vāmana** the fifth main incarnation of Viṣṇu, as a dwarf. He took this form to recover the universe from the demon Bali, who had gained control over it, by obtaining a boon from him which would give him the rule over as much space as he could cover in three steps. Viṣṇu then changed into a giant and in three strides covered the whole of creation.

***vānaprastha*** forest dweller, hermit; the fourth stage of life in the Hindu system of *āśrama dharma* which could be shared by husband and wife.

**Varāha** the third main incarnation of Viṣṇu, as a boar, which he undertook when the demon Hiraṇyākṣa tossed the earth into the cosmic ocean. He killed the demon, plunged into the ocean and brought the earth up on his tusks. In his iconographical representations he usually has a human body and a boar's head and carries a small figure of the Earth goddess on his shoulder or arm.

**Vārāṇasī** (vern. Banāras, anglicized as Benares) in ancient times known as Kāśī and a famous centre of Brahminic learning, it is one of the most sacred cities and places of pilgrimage for Hindus, situated as it is on the north (left) bank of the sacred river Gaṅgā. It is sacred particularly to Śiva and made famous especially by its many bathing *ghāṭs*, frequented daily by pilgrims from all over India, and by the palaces built above them.

***varṇa*** colour; the Skt. name for the original four castes.

**Varuṇa** in the Vedas he is the high god of the encompassing sky (cf. the Gr. Uranos) and in the RV still bears the title of Asura in its original sense of high god (cf. Av. Ahura Mazdā). He is the first-born son of Aditi and thus the first ruler of the universe and the all-seeing guardian of *ṛta*, the cosmic law, both natural and moral. Skies and cosmic space being regarded as the cosmic ocean, he is also the god of waters and rules the seas, his vehicle or mount being a fish or a *makara*. Mitra is his close associate and when they share the domain of the world, Varuṇa rules by night and Mitra, as a solar deity, rules by day. Varuṇa's status as a high god later declined and he is now only a minor god in Hinduism.

***vāsanā*** indwelling impression, tendency, karmic seed. It refers to traces of past actions and ties in a person's character which stem from his previous lives.

**Vasanta** spring; goddess of spring (cf. Slav. Vesna).

**Vasiṣṭha** the name of a Vedic seer and of several later sages, among them the teacher of the system of Yoga Vāsiṣṭha.

**Vāsudeva** one of the names of Viṣṇu (as Kṛṣṇa).

**Vāsuki** the king of the *nāgas*, the serpent-beings of the deep. He was used by the gods and *asuras* when they churned the cosmic ocean to obtain the drink of immortality. Some Purāṇas identify him with Viṣṇu's snake Śeṣa/Ananta.

**Vāta** see Vāyu.

**Vātsyāyana** (fourth or fifth century A.D.) the author of Kāma Sūtra, the textbook of love.

***vāyu*** wind; air as one of the four (or five) elements.

**Vāyu**, also: Vāta the god of wind and the 'breath of gods' who mysteriously penetrates all dimensions of existence. In Vedic times it was believed that he could bestow longer life on his worshippers and even grant immortality. He ruled the life force manifested as breath which was then called *ātman* (cf. Gr. *atmos*), but when *ātman* came to be regarded as the highest principle in the Upaniṣads, the term *prāṇa* became current for the life force. In the Purāṇas Vāyu is also the king of the *gandharvas*.

**Veda** (knowledge) a summary name for the sacred scriptures of Hinduism, regarded by the orthodoxy as divine revelation (*śruti*) and comprising the four Vedas or collections of hymns (Ṛg Veda, Sāma Veda, Yajur Veda and Atharva Veda Saṃhitās), the Brāhmaṇas or priestly treatises, the Āraṇyakes or forest books and the Upaniṣads or philosophical and mystical treatises.

**Vedāṅgas** textbooks of auxiliary branches of Vedic knowledge, six in number: phonetics (*śikṣā*), metre (*chandas*), grammar (*vyākaraṇa*), etymology (*nirukta*), astronomy/astrology (*jyotiṣa*) and ritual (*kalpa*).

**Vedānta** ('end of the Veda') a designation for the Upaniṣads as the last portion of the sacred scriptures of the Veda recognized in Hinduism as divine revelation (*śruti*), which may also be understood in the sense that they are divinely inspired or derived from inner experience of the ultimate divine reality on the part of those who produced them; also: a designation for the philosophy derived from Upaniṣadic thought. The main message of Vedānta is the essential identity between the self and the divine source of the world which is, in a popularized form ('the Divine or God dwells in everybody and in everything'), the most widespread view of the world among Hindus. In the context of systematic Indian thought it is one of the six 'orthodox' doctrinal traditions of Hindu philosophy, also called Uttara Mīmāṁsā, There are three main schools within the Vedāntic tradition itself (and a few minor schools or subschools), with three main protagonists: Advaita or non-dual school (Śaṅkara), Viṣiṣṭa Advaita or 'qualified' non-dual teaching (Rāmānuja) and Dvaita or the school of dualism (Madhva). But even Madhva accepted the dependence on God of the world and of all beings. All three protagonists used extensively (and often rather selectively) quotations from the Upaniṣads in trying to prove the correctness of their respective stances.

***vedi*** the sacrificial altar.

**Vedic language** the archaic form of Sanskrit preserved in the Vedic hymns which is not, strictly speaking, a direct ancestor of the Sanskrit of the Upaniṣads, but something like a parallel dialect to the ancestor language of the Upaniṣads. Therefore some philologists call it Old Indian (OI) or Old Indo-Āryan (OIA) rather than Old Sanskrit.

**Vedism** a Western term for the stage of Indian religion prevailing during the time of the creation of the Ṛgvedic hymns up to about 900 B.C. It was succeeded by the period of Brāhmanism dominated by the supremacy of the priestly caste and a build-up of ritualism.

***videha*** bodyless; *videhamukti*: liberation on physical death.

***vidyā*** knowledge, wisdom. In the context of religious and philosophical texts it usually denotes direct knowledge of the transcendent reality resulting from yogic insight which dispels ignorance (*avidyā*), the condition of the untrained mind.

***vidyādhara(s)*** ('bearers of knowledge') in iconography: graceful flying (but wingless) attendants or aerial spirits on icons of deities and saints of Hinduism as well as Buddhism and Jainism. They often hold swords symbolizing knowledge which cuts through ignorance, and garlands symbolizing victory over evil.

***vijaya*** hemp, *Cannabis indica.*

**Vijayā** (victorious) a name of Durgā.

**Vijayanagar** ('the city of victory') the last stronghold of Hinduism against the Muslim conquest, a kingdom founded by a Hindu confederacy in South India around 1336 which withstood the numerous onslaughts of Islamic forces for almost 300 years and was instrumental in rescuing some important features of Hinduism from obliteration.

***vijñānamaya kośa*** ('consciousness-made sheath') a Vedāntic term for the higher mental body in the system of five sheaths, the other four *kośas* being: *annamaya*, *prāṇamaya*, *manomaya* and *ānandamaya.*

**Vikramāditya** (Pkt. Vikramjit) a title assumed by Chandra Gupta II (376–415 A.D.), who defeated the Śaka invaders, and possibly by one or two other later Gupta rulers who had to fight off Hun invasions. (Its meaning, 'sun's progress', suggests a victorious and unstoppable force and therefore the title came to be circulated as a name of a heroic legendary king in popular stories.) Kālidāsa is believed to have lived at the court of Chandra Gupta II for some time.

***vīṇa*** an ancient musical instrument, originally a kind of harp, later lute. It has several variants.

**Vināyaka** the name of Gaṇeśa as remover of obstacles.

***vīra*** hero; spiritual giant; accomplished person. According to Vedic mythological view, given special prominence especially in connection with the Indo-Āryan conquest of India, war heroes were transported by *apsarases* directly to Indra's heaven, an obviously archaic IE popular belief (cf. Valkyries, performing the same function in Germ. mythology from where it got into Wagner's operatic Ring cycle).

***virāj*** m.: king, monarch, sovereign; n.: universal sovereignty; in the AV (f): a mysterious cosmic force, sometimes identified with the cosmic cow and with Vāk (Vāc). The sun and moon are described as her calves.

**Vīraśaivas** members of a South Indian sect marked by devotional worship of Śiva as 'hero'. It overlaps with Liṅgāyatism.

**Virocana** a foremost *asura* who, at the same time as Indra, sought to discover the nature of his self (*ātman*). Told by Prajāpati that it was what one saw reflected on the surface of water, Virocana was satisfied with the explanation and thus became a protagonist of materialism, later expounded by Cārvāka. But Indra was not satisfied and, inquiring further until he obtained instruction about where the real truth lay, became the archetype of the genuine seeker after the ultimate truth (a story told in CU 8,7–12, which found its conclusion in Buddhist Pl. sources where Indra, although being the king of the gods, became the follower of the Buddha and reached the first stage of sainthood which guarantees the eventual attainment of liberation).

***viśuddha*** (purified) ***cakra*** in the system of Kuṇḍalinī Yoga it is the spiritual centre in the subtle body opposite the throat in the shape of a sixteen-petalled lotus.

**Viṣiṣṭa Advaita** the 'qualified' non-dual teaching of Rāmānuja according to which *brahman*, the ultimate reality, is also the Supreme Lord, the personal God who exists from eternity. He created the world out of his own subtle body by transforming it into a gross one. He cannot, however, prevent his gross body (the world) from developing blemishes (suffering, evil). The motivation for the creation is said to be, as in most Vedāntic sources, God's spontaneous, creative playfulness (*līlā*). Individual beings are described as off-shoots or 'attributes' of God. Yet they also have their own self-conscious existence and this is preserved to them even after they reach liberation. The way to liberation, for the followers of the school, is surrender to God on a path of devotion leading to a mystic union with God in *bhakti* (although not dissolving in him), which is in part dependent on God's grace (*prasāda*), but has to be accompanied by the removal of ignorance (*avidyā*) on the part of the follower. Rāmānuja identified the Supreme Lord with Viṣṇu and his philosophy became the basis for Vaiṣṇava theology.

**Viṣṇu** from a solar deity in the Vedas with certain indications that he also represented spiritual enlightenment, he became one of the three gods of the Hindu Trinity (Trimurti) as God the Preserver who sustains creation during the time of its duration and incarnates from time to time into it to assist gods or mankind when they are in need. In the teachings of his sectarian worshippers he came to be regarded as the highest deity and the sole source of manifestation. This particular role of his is expressed symbolically in his mythological form as Anantaśāyin, i.e. reclining on Ananta, the 'serpent of eternity' (also called Śeṣa) and floating on the cosmic waters which harbour the unmanifest reality. His creative potency is shown in this image by a lotus growing out of his navel and his supremacy or universal lordship by the image of Brahma sitting on the lotus, prepared to execute the process of creation as Viṣṇu's subordinate. In his active form Viṣṇu moves about riding on his mount Garuḍa, a mythical bird-like creature, sometimes portrayed as half human. His wife is Lakṣmī and sometimes also Sarasvatī. At the end of the world period he brings about the emanation from his forehead of Śiva, who then destroys the universe by means of his cosmic dance. After Viṣṇu has had a period of rest on his snake couch, during which he is united with the goddess Yoganidrā, the process of creation starts all over again.

**Viśvakarman** ('all-maker') in earlier Vedic literature sometimes described as the demiurge, i.e. the fashioner of the universe, a subordinate agent in the process of creation, he becomes in later mythology the chief architect and artificer of the gods.

**Viśvedevas** ('all gods') a summary designation of lower deities or of a group of minor gods; the communal god of village folks.

**Vivasvant** ('brilliant') an epithet of Sūrya, sometimes addressed as a separate solar deity, one of the larger group of Ādityas.

***viveka*** discrimination (between what is substantial and what is unsubstantial, real and illusory, true and false), an important quality to be developed in the *jñāna* approach to the realization of the final goal; *vivekin*: one who has developed the quality; an advanced *jñānayogi*.

**Vivekananda** (1863–1902; his orig. name was Narendranāth Datta) the founder of the Ramakrishna Order of *saṁnyāsis* and of the Ramakrishna Mission. As a young intellectual he first joined the Brāhmo Samāj, but when he met Ramakrishna, he experienced a mystical state when Ramakrishna touched him with his foot, and became his disciple. He represented Hinduism with his modern version of the Vedānta message at the first 'Parliament of Religions' in Chicago 1893 and was highly acclaimed there. He then travelled widely in the USA and Europe, lecturing on Vedāntic philosophy and the practice of Rāja Yoga as a way to salvation. His influence is still felt both in India and in the Western circles of the followers of yoga practice.

**Vrātya** one bound by a vow (*vrata*); the designation for early Indo-Āryan, but non-Vedic, combatant fraternities in North East India (which eventually became the ancient kingdom of Magadha, now Bihār and West Bengal). They are likely to have been the first adventurous Āryans to enter India from Iran and migrated further east to what later became Magadha under the pressure of subsequent waves of Āryan immigrants who then created the Vedic civilization in Saptasindhu. The Vrātyas possessed an ancient religious and spiritual tradition of their own which was later brahmanized and codified in the AV when the Vedic civilization spilled over from Saptasindhu and incorporated Magadha. From their midst had emerged the so-called *ekavrātyas* or solitary wanderers who had a reputation as saints or accomplished adepts, even in the Vedic territory, and wandering teams of three, consisting of an experienced older master (*māgadha*), a pupil (*brahmacāri*) and a young female attendant (*puṁścalī*). These Vrātya teams often wandered into the heartland of the early Vedic civilization in Saptasindhu and performed magic and fertility rites for the population which involved invocations and probably also song and dance as well as ritual copulation in the fields. These teams may well have been a factor among other precursors of Tantric sects and movements which emerged in later centuries. The present-day Bāuls, who have clear Tantric associations and often also travel in similar teams of three, are possibly descended from them. The original combatant Vrātya (=sworn) fraternities can possibly be seen as of IE origin if one can go by similarities with fraternities of young combatant men in ancient Greece known as *kourētes*. After the brahmanization of Magadha many Vrātyas with a spiritual background were accepted into the caste system as brahmins, the combatant élite became *kṣatriyas* and most of the rest merged with *vaiśyas*, but those who remained strongly committed to their ancient Vrātya traditions continued their itinerant vocation and were designated in Brahminic sources as 'renegade' or 'degenerate' Āryans who refused to recognize the Vedic rituals.

**Vṛndāvana** (Vrindavan, Brindaban) the once forested area near Mathurā, the scene of Kṛṣṇa's youthful pranks, heroic deeds and dalliances with the *gopīs*. It is now a town and a centre of pilgrimages and has many *aśrams* concentrating on various forms of the practice of *bhaktimārga* and shrines and temples dedicated to Kṛṣṇa worship. A part of the periodic festival events is a ceremonial re-enactment of incidents from his life and a popular part of a pilgrim's progress is a round of visits to the places where these legendary events are believed to have taken place.

**Vṛtra, Vṛtrāsura** the primeval demon-snake or dragon, the Vedic adversary of Indra, symbolizing inertia and stagnation in life. In the cosmic context he stands for the precreational unmanifest reality or primeval chaos which harbours in itself the potential manifestation or cosmos. In the Vedic myth Vṛtra held captive the fruitful waters of life (which are in the context of the myth synonymous with maidens or virgins). Indra attacked the dragon and, having pierced him with his spear, freed the maidens and impregnated them, thereby starting the process of creation or manifestation of the universe. This is a creation myth with roots in ancient IE mythology as indicated by surviving European folk tales about the knight in shining armour who killed a dragon and freed the captive princess, marrying her and winning a kingdom. (It is also reflected in the legend of St. George. Cf. also Gr. legends about Theseus and Ariadne and particularly about

Perseus and Andromeda.) The demon-like and seemingly negative role of Vṛtra should not be interpreted as a total negation of life or existence or as the embodiment of evil. Rather he represents the other party in the polarity which is basic to reality pulsating between existence and non-existence, emanation and withdrawal. The designation of Vṛtra as an *asura* gives him, in ancient Vedic understanding, an equal status with the high gods. Thus Indra as the active and Vṛtra as the passive principle in the process of creation clearly represent what later sources describe as *sṛṣṭi* (manifestation of the universe). They also represent what Purāṇic mythology calls the Brahma's day and night or what, in a wider context, it sees as a Brahma's whole lifespan during which the creation pulsates between periods of expansion and rest and the great cosmic night during which all creation is withdrawn into the transcendent source before a new Brahma is born. The ceaseless and repetitive nature of this gigantic process is foreshadowed in the Vedic myth by the fact that the Indra-Vṛtra combat is portrayed as a recurring event since Vṛtra, like the high gods, can never be entirely killed or if he is killed, he is immediately reborn. The event was remembered every morning when night gave way to day and was celebrated at every winter solstice so that, in a way, it is still with us as New Year celebrations. On another level the myth was later interpreted as the drama of the coming of the monsoon rains, when Vṛtra in the shape of clouds holds back the life-giving waters and Indra's spear (lightning) pierces him and releases them, making the earth fruitful and causing new growth of vegetation.

**Vyāsa** ('arranger'), also: Vedavyāsa the traditional name for the unknown redactor(s) of the Veda. The redaction or final fixing of the RV is believed to have taken place around 1000 B.C. under unknown circumstances, and that of SV and YV some time in the course of the subsequent two or three centuries. The AV was arranged in the course of the brahmanization of Vrātya lore, probably in the sixth century B.C. The expression came to be regarded as a personal name and Vyāsa came to be seen as the mythical compiler of many important works of Hinduism such as the Mahābhārata, Purāṇas and some commentaries. He is called Kṛṣṇa Dvaipāyana in the Mhb, because he was dark (*kṛṣṇa*) and brought up on an island (*dvīpa*) in the Yamunā. Some Purāṇas, however, list several Vyāsas as incarnations of Brahma or Viṣṇu for the purpose of arranging the scriptures.

***vyāvahārika*** relating to the world (of *māyā*); phenomenal.

***vyūha*** appearance; manifestation or emanation of God; a technical term in the Pañcarātra system for the manifestations of Viṣṇu on earth as the Supreme God with his divine essence fully present (which may be seen as a kind of upgrading of the *avatāra* doctrine). He has four great emanations: as Vāsudeva, Saṁkarṣaṇa, Pradyumna and Aniruddha as well as their respective sub-emanations in this elaborate system which also adopted some traditional *avatāras* and adapted their status to its theories.

**Water** one of the four (or five) cosmic elements and a symbol of purity as well as fruitfulness and also of the mental process; See Āpas and Bath, and cf. Churning the ocean.

**Wheel** (*cakra*) an important multi-faceted symbol in Hinduism with solar associations. It represents the ceaseless round of rebirths and the ever-revolving or pulsating saṁsāric universe, with its ceaselessly revolving wheel of righteousness (*dharmacakra*) which secures the round of punishments (*daṇḍacakra*) where deserved. The axis of the wheel symbol represents the *axis mundi* and points to the existence of the passage beyond the revolving wheel of existence into the transcendent centre of tranquillity. All this is also symbolized by Kṛṣṇa's circular *rāsa-līlā* dance in which he whirls around from *gopī* to *gopī*, while remaining unaffected in his divine nature in the centre. This image of Kṛṣṇa's circular dance with the *gopīs* is in turn symbolical of God playfully creating the world and participating in it in a multifarious fashion as the inner self of his creatures who are joined with him on the path of *bhakti* in a rapturous mystic union. The wheel also represents the cyclic nature of time (*kālacakra*) and also the all-round power of a world-governing monarch (*cakravartin*). It is further reflected ritually in the circumambulation (*pradakṣina*) of shrines in individual worship and re-appears in some rituals as the *maṇḍala* diagram, used also for meditational purposes and representing both the universe and the human personality as well as showing the way beyond.

**Widow** (*vidhavā*) widowhood has always had a certain stigma of guilt attached to it in Hinduism and there has always been at the very least an ambiguous attitude to the remarriage of widows. In Vedic times, and up to the epic time, levirate (*niyoga* – marrying the brother-in-law or his next-of-kin to produce offspring on behalf of the deceased one) was possible and normal remarriage occurred sporadically where brahmin orthodoxy did not have a firm grip. Most Dharma Śāstras forbid it, however, and as a consequence, as the grip of Brahminic orthodoxy tightened, the widow sank to a very low subordinate position in the family which could be avoided only by following the husband onto the funeral pyre (see *satī*). Some remnants of this attitude to widows still persist in Hinduism today, despite more than a hundred years of efforts at reform, and modern legislation.

**Worship** (*pūj*ā) an act of reverential attention and personal aspiration turned towards the transcendent or God either directly or through the medium of an image or a symbol (*pratīka*) by way of a material (ritual) or a mental (meditational) procedure or a combination of both. The symbol may be natural (the sun, a tree, a stone) or artificial (an emblem or an effigy – *mūrti*). Less often, and then mainly in the meditational approach, it may even be purely mental: either conceptual (the Lord – *īśvara*, i.e. *saguṇa brahman*, e.g. as Kṛṣṇa) or 'abstract' (the ultimate reality, i.e. *nirguṇa brahman*, e.g. *ātman*, the inner self). Such highly advanced meditational procedures are invariably preceded by the employment of concrete symbols, natural or 'artificial', or even by ritual *pūjā* involving the use of concrete symbols. The concept of 'idols', still employed by some authors with respect to Hindu worship, was unknown to Hinduism and the very idea of worshipping 'idols' is alien to it. It was coined by early uncomprehending Western observers unaware of the deep and rather sophisticated background to Hindu religious observances. Much of this wide and deep context of Hinduism is in some way present at the back of the minds of even simple Hindu folks, conveyed to them through the numerous myths and legends.

**Yādavas** an ancient Indo-Āryan tribe.

***yajña*** oblation, sacrifice; worship by making an offering to the gods to ensure prosperity, well-being and offspring as well as to sustain the gods in their continuous task of maintaining the world in existence. This indicates the mutuality and the magic nature of the sacrificial ritual which presumes to parallel the process of world creation through the sacrifice of the cosmic *puruśa*, as described in one of the myths of creation (RV 10,90; cf. Sacrifice). Offerings are also made to or on behalf of deceased ancestors to sustain them in their blessed state in the afterlife or to help them along on their passage to further lives.

**Yājñavalkya** the mythical compiler of YV–VS; the later supposed author of a *smṛti* bearing the name. By far the most interesting person of this name bearing some marks of a real person was, however, the learned brahmin of the BU who won many disputations about the nature of the highest reality (*brahman*/*ātman*) and other topics in gatherings at the court of king Janaka. At the peak of his career he renounced worldly life to become a mendicant, leaving his riches to one of his two wives and expounding his teaching to the other one, who was not interested in worldly possessions, but asked for his wisdom.

**Yajur Veda** (YV) the third collection of Vedic scriptures which deals with sacrificial procedures and formulae. It has two versions, the so-called Black collection or Taittirīya Saṁhitā (TS) and the White collection known as Vājasaneyī Saṁhitā (VS), which do not differ substantially from each other.

***yajus*** sacrificial formula.

***yakṣa*** (f. *yakṣī*) godling, sprite; a category of nature spirits of vegetation or a kind of lower deity, often residing in trees and frequenting fields and forests. They are usually benevolent towards humans if propitiated and are believed to be able to grant offspring to barren women. Their popularity led to their adoption also by Buddhism and Jainism in their iconography. Their ruler is Kubera whose mount (*vāhana*) is a dwarf *yakṣa*.

***yama*** (self-)control, restraint; the first part of Patañjali's *aṣṭaṅga yoga*, i.e. the observance of *ahiṁsā* (non-violence), *satya* (truthfulness), *asteya* (non-stealing), *brahmacarya* (pure living) and *aparigraha* (non-acquisitiveness).

**Yama** the mythical first man in one version of the origin of mankind, who produced the human race with his twin sister Yamī. As the first man to die, he became the ruler of the realm of the dead and also their judge, sending them to different regions according to their merit. His mount is a black buffalo.

**Yamunā** (Jumna) a sacred river, a tributary of Gaṅgā, joining it at Prayāga; as goddess she is regarded as the daughter of the Sun god.

***yantra*** tool, instrument, surgical tool, atronomical sextant, mechanical device; diagram; magic drawing used to ward off evil forces; symbolical depiction of the universe or human personality used for meditation in some forms of yoga.

**Yaśodā** a *gopī*, the wife of the cowherd Nanda who became the foster-mother of Kṛṣṇa.

***yati*** one who practises a discipline; an ascetic.

**Yavanas** The Skt. name for Greeks.

***yoga***, **yoga** a systematic discipline which includes a technique for the mastery of the bodily organism and for rendering it healthy (Hatha Yoga) and various methods or techniques of mind training for the sake of gaining the final knowledge and liberation. According to the Hindu religious tradition it was revealed to man by *īśvara* (the Lord) and even gods gained immortality and their supreme powers by its practice (the legendary story of churning the cosmic ocean to obtain the drink of immortality being a mythological image for the technique of yoga meditation). In the course of elaboration of yoga techniques over the centuries some of these techniques came to be regarded as dominant or chief factors in a particular approach to the goal and developed into separate systematic yoga disciplines, e.g. Kuṇḍalinī Yoga, using refined Hatha Yoga techniques to awaken spiritual centres in the subtle body; Bhakti Yoga, making the main vehicle of progress the devotion to God; Karma Yoga, with its emphasis on disinterested action; Jñāna Yoga, stressing the role of direct inner knowledge, and others, to say nothing of the extraordinary, and possibly controversial, development represented by Tantra Yoga. All these so-called Yogas overlap in certain basic requirements, e.g. moral discipline (the rules of which may vary, at least in some of the schools), single-minded concentration and elimination of ignorance. Most of them, to a greater or lesser degree, also share important procedures with the Classical Yoga of Patañjali. Nevertheless, fragmentation and a loss of an over-all purpose did occur as some schools were sidetracked and concentrated on partial achievements brought about by their particular techniques. This led to efforts to re-emphasize the spiritual purpose of yoga and a new term was coined, namely Raja Yoga (associated with Vivekananda's name), in which, however, the component of Hatha Yoga received too little attention. Aurobindo redefined the spiritual path, on the basis of his global outlook aiming at the spiritualization of the universe, as Integral Yoga. On the whole, however, it would seem that the Classical Yoga of Patañjali offers even now a broad and reliable basis, a global approach in methodology as well as the highest possible spiritual outlook for the individual.

**Yoga** one of the six systems of Hindu philosophy (*darśaṇas*), which includes the eightfold yoga path (see *aṣṭaṅga yoga*) for the achievement of liberation, expounded in Patañjali's *Yoga Sūtras*.

***yoganidrā*** 'yogic sleep', an absorbed state of consciousness; Viṣṇu's state of mind, said to be his union with the goddess Yoganidrā, when he is resting on his snake Śeṣa between the dissolution of one universe and the manifestation of the next.

**Yoga Vāsiṣṭha** the school of philosophy and yoga practice which grew out of the sectarian cult of Rāma in an attempt to match the success of the Kṛṣṇa cult associated with the yoga methods expounded by him in the BhG. Philosophically it developed into a kind of Advaita Vedānta school which is not dissimilar to that of Śaṅkara and which was influenced, as was Śaṅkara, but far more visibly, by the Buddhist notion of emptiness (*śūnyatā*). Its practice has the characteristics of the path of Jñāna Yoga with great stress on meditation (*dhyāna*) amidst active life which is reminiscent of the Karma Yoga path of the BhG. The school probably started developing already in the sixth century A.D. and later produced its own path of Bhakti Yoga.

**Yogi, yogin** one who practises some form of yoga.

***yoginī*** an initiated female partner in Tantric *maithuna* practice; a witch with magic powers. The term is also used in *śakti* cults for a group of female deities in the retinue of Durgā.

***yoni*** ('holder', 'receptacle') womb, vagina. Its effigy was found and identified as such in Harappan excavations, but there are no references to it as an object of worship in the Vedas. It emerged in that capacity in Hinduism with *śakti* cults and, in combination with the *liṅga*, in the cult of Śiva. Symbolically, it represents in the Tantric context the potent void in which all things are inherent and from which they emerge in the process of manifestation.

***yuga*** age, in the sense of a legendary historical period; there are four main ages, with conditions of living progressively deteriorating: Kṛta Yuga (accomplished age), Tretā Yuga, Dvāpara Yuga (these two names appear to be derived from the throw of three and two in the game of dice) and the present one, Kali Yuga (often called the dark age, but probably also derived from the dice game as the throw of one, which is called the 'loser'). They more or less correspond to the Golden, Silver, Heroic (Copper or Bronze) and Iron ages of Graeco-Roman mythology.

***yūpa*** sacrificial post, used since early Vedic times and later transformed into the flagpole (*dhvaja*) outside temples. It is symbolical of Indra's banner and the spear with which he pierced Vṛtra and propped up heaven to keep it and earth apart, and hence also of the 'cosmic pillar' or world axis, with further associations with respect to *śivaliṅga*.

**Zarathushtra** (Gr. Zoroaster) the prophet who reformed Iranian religion before 1100 B.C., thereby parting it from its ancient Indo-Iranian form and its close correspondence with the ancient Vedic religion. In spite of that, many ideas can still be detected in the Zoroastrian scripture Avesta which parallel Vedism. The Avestan language (Av.) is closely akin to Vedic.

**Zero** was invented in India, according to indirect evidence, quite early, but the earliest record comes from A.D. 595. Its discovery may have had some connection with speculations about the 'potent void' or vice versa (cf. *śūnya* and *śūnyatā*) as there is a kind of similarity between them: although 'void' of any intrinsic value of its own, zero has the potential of upgrading other numerals that are joined to it. It has been said that whoever was responsible for the discovery of the zero was in greatness among men second only to the Buddha.

**Zodiac** was adopted by Indian astrologers in the early centuries of our era under Greek influence, but not universally, and often alongside the Indian system of *nakṣatras*. Both systems seem to have coexisted to the present day.